THE PRODUCTIVITY EPIPHANY

THE PRODUCTIVITY EPIPHANY:

LEADING EDGE IDEAS ON TIME MANAGEMENT, SELF MANAGEMENT, COMMUNICATION AND BECOMING MORE PRODUCTIVE IN ANY AREA OF LIFE!

VINCENT HARRIS

BECKWORTH PUBLICATIONS

THE PRODUCTIVITY EPIPHANY Copyright © 2008 by Vincent Harris

ISBN: 978-0-9818791-0-9

BECKWORTH PUBLICATIONS
3108 E. 10th Street
Trenton, MO 64683
www.BeckworthPublications.com
Email: Admin@beckworthpublications.com

Ordering Information:
Quantity sales. Special discounts are available on quantity purchases by corporations, associations, and others. For details, contact the "Special Sales Department at Beckworth Publications.

Beckworth Publications and the Beckworth Publications logo are trademarks of Beckworth Publications.

Printed in the United States of America.

Library of Congress Cataloging-in-Publication Data
Harris, Vincent
        The Productivity Epiphany: Leading Edge Ideas: Time Management, Self Management, Communication. Become More Productive in Any Area of Life! / by Vincent Harris
Library of Congress Control Number: 2008910283

Copyediting and proofreading by Connie Akers.

Book design by Brion Sausser

Praise for THE PRODUCTIVITY EPIPHANY

"*The Productivity Epiphany* provides a steady stream of thought provoking insights you can use to ramp up your productivity in all areas of life. It's full of unusual and unpredictable insights and tools, yet written in a way that will comfortably jar your mind into new ways of perceiving and understanding. This is one book you can't afford to be without."

Mollie Marti, Ph.D. CEO, Best Life Design, and Author of *The 12 Factors of Business Success*

The Productivity Epiphany is bursting with insights that will allow you to be more productive and get more enjoyment out of life. Vince Harris shares the wisdom that is the result of hundreds of coaching sessions with his clients over the last decade-and much, much more. This book belongs in your personal development library!

Dr. Joe Vitale, Author of *The Attractor Factor* www.mrfire.com

"59 specific ways to influence others, yourself and your life! Vince has put together a life manual that cuts through the BS that a lot of books are filled with. What you get here is a quick idea, why it works and how to use it! Many of these ideas you can apply in the next few minutes and get a measurable result for yourself. I really like the way Vince talks in plain language that anyone can understand and therefore apply! If you are looking for that "Life Manual" you can take with you as well as to the bank, this is it! It's a home run, Vince, great job!"

Harlan Goerger, President H. Goerger & Associates, Author of *The Selling Gap*

"Our happiness, productivity, fulfillment, self-esteem level, charisma quotient, and ability to manifest the things most important to us are all dependent upon how we picture ourselves, others and the world in general. If we can alter how we perceive things, we can shift our reality and experience new insights and breakthroughs in every aspect of our lives. *The Productivity Epiphany* is loaded with wisdom, new ways to see ourselves and others, and entertaining stories that allow us to see things in an entirely new and supportive light. If you are ready to experience a bunch of epiphanies of your own, this is the book for you."

Dr. Joe Rubino, Founder, www.centerforpersonalreinvention.com, and www.selfesteemsystem.com

"My humble library is simply awash with books on sales and self improvement. I bought some of them, but most were sent by friends and acquaintances wanting an endorsement. I haven't read most of them, but I'm reading this one and I'll tell you why. It's eminently readable.

The first thing I noticed is that there are a few more than 59 chapters populating a few more than 200 pages. My rudimentary math tells me the average chapter is about 2 pages long and I can handle that. It's ideal for those few moments I can scrape out of my day, like the bathroom, for example.

The next thing I noticed is that it is largely comprised of stories and they are *good* stories. Stories are the best way to learn.

Here's the bottom line. Books you don't read can't possibly do you any good. *The Productivity Epiphany* will help you improve your life because you will read it and enjoy it in the process."

Hank Trisler, Author of *NO BULL SELLING* and *NO BULL SALES MANAGEMENT*, both published by Bantam Books, NY, NY.

"*The Productivity Epiphany* shows us that becoming more effective in life doesn't always come down to a single formula; huge leaps forward often result from those "ah ha" moments that seem to come from nowhere. When you read Vince's book, you'll know where your epiphanies came from!"

Tom Antion, Past President: National Capital Speakers Association, and Author of *The Ultimate Guide to Electronic Marketing for Small Business*

"This book is jam packed with useful tools! Vince Harris provides dozens and dozens of fascinating and practical techniques to increase our influence and effectiveness. Harris finds these tools in scientific research literature, his personal experience, or the proven experience of others, and presents them in an engaging, informative, and easy style. I was absorbed and expanded by this book. You will profit from owning, reading, and re-reading this book."

Eric S. Knowles, Emeritus Professor of Psychology, University of Arkansas, Chief Scientist, Omega Change Consulting Group, and Author of *Resistance and Persuasion*

"Insightful, Engaging and Informative! Vince Harris's new book *"The Productivity Epiphany"* is truly a blueprint on how to master your time, your relationships and your life. The wisdom you will gain from reading this book will give you the courage to change your life and the strategies to take your life to the next level of understanding and success."

Johnny 'The Transition Man' Campbell, Author of *Selling to Brand X & Y* - WWW.TRANSITIONMAN.COM

"If you are truly ready to transcend your past limitations and create extraordinary success for your life, The Productivity Epiphany is the resource you need. Providing you with life-transforming information, new levels of self awareness and actionable strategies, it will empower you to start becoming the productive person you deserve to be!"

Hal 'Yo Pal' Elrod, Author of TAKING LIFE HEAD ON! and Co-founder of Your Best Life Coaching - WWW.YOURBESTLIFEEVERYDAY.COM

"Vince Harris has brought together a collection of advice and ideas which if applied can have a positive impact on its reader. The ideas included are presented in a way that is unique and easy to digest."

Josh Hinds, Speaker, Author, and Entrepreneur - WWW.GETMOTIVATION.COM

CONTENTS

Dedication

To my daughter Chloe, a beautiful little girl with a brilliant mind. There's nothing you could do to make me love you any more, and nothing you could do to make me love you any less.

FOREWORD

It's the greatest challenge we all face. Getting ourselves to do things we want to do but can't get past the inertia to build momentum…to actually do those things.

The second problem we face? The one that happens when we actually DO get up the initiative, we do build momentum to face overwhelm and moments…and weeks that tax us. What do we typically do? We tend to give up doing that which we want and revert to that which we have done. That could be our old job, old career, old business, old any-thing…and we let go of that which is unfamiliar. Why?

We have evolved consistently over millennia to do that which keeps us alive…that which causes us to survive. And that is a very good thing. But there is no gene that allows for initiative. Safety, security, love, ac-quisition, eating, physical activity…yes. Initiative and stick-to-itiveness are very different. We aren't wired for it.

Instead, we are wired to be comfortable. We are wired to have enough. So we face ourselves and only ourselves. We face our most complex de-sires and emotions and they don't want to move, they don't want to manage time effectively. And, it is the "thinking you" that can win over your basest drives and desires.

Don't get me wrong, your drives and desires are good things. But they've been running the brain for so long that the brain forgot it could take control.

The brain can consciously help you lose weight, get things done and in general change. Consciousness is strong but nonconsciousness usually wins out because conscious strength needs to be trained to win the "friendly battle" with the no conscious.

Vince Harris, in this brilliant new book is going to show you how to do just that.

I'm delighted that you have taken the initiative today.

My hat is off to you and I am excited for you as you begin this wonderful journey.

–Kevin Hogan, Psy.D., Author of *The Psychology of Persuasion*

ACKNOWLEDGEMENTS

My parents, Jerry Harris and Cheryl Mclain, first and foremost, got me here. They successfully did the toughest job around; they made sure I made it from infancy to adulthood in one piece, and believe me, I didn't make that an easy task. To my parents, I love you.

In the summer of 1976, a neighbor and family friend, Wayne Brassfield, gave me a tattered copy of the classic self-help book *Think and Grow Rich*. To say that this single decision by Wayne changed my life would be an understatement. But then again, that's just Wayne. He's made a habit of positively impacting the lives of young people. Thank you Wayne.

In 1980, Bob Timmons, the track coach for the Kansas Jay-hawks, and mentor to Jim Ryun, took the time to write and send me two inspirational letters. They came at a time when I really needed them. Somehow, I think he knew that. One evening, some 26 years after I had received the last of those two letters, I called him to say "Thank you!" It was an emotional evening for both of us.

INTRODUCTION

"An artist's duty is rather to stay open-minded and in a state where he can receive information and inspiration. You always have to be ready for that little artistic Epiphany."

-Nick Cave

EPIPHANY:

1): a usually sudden manifestation or perception of the essential nature or meaning of something **(2):** an intuitive grasp of reality through something (as an event) usually simple and striking **(3):** an illuminating discovery, realization, or disclosure b: a revealing scene or moment.

Maybe you can recall the last time you experienced an epiphany. While the experience certainly creates a profound sense of mental clarity, where only seconds before, confusion had been clouding your mind, the most defining aspect of an epiphany is a distinctly different set of physical sensations. A strange combination of surprise, elation, and gratitude, all wrapped into one wonderfully freeing feeling. In that moment, the physical boundaries that usually define where your sense of self begins and ends vanish into thin air. You feel connected to some vast storehouse of wisdom that has suddenly allowed you to understand, in a way you would find hard to describe at first, the solution to some issue or challenge that, until now, had seemed insurmountable.

Even more surprising, perhaps, is the fact that the person, event, thought or information that serve as the trigger for our epiphanies, often have no apparent logical connection to the problem we've been so desperately seeking to resolve. Here lies the secret. Because we are doing or thinking about something that has no conceivable correlation to our "problem", the rigid perceptual filters that normally keep us fixated in a way that only allows us to see the "obstacles" between us and the desired solution, have temporarily ceased to exist. Our open mindedness lets the information slip past the gatekeeper of our mind, sliding like some ethereal skeleton key into our mental deadbolt. Then, with one easy turn, "click", the door swings wide open, and we breathe a heavy sigh of relief.

The Productivity Epiphany was written to provide you with stories, insights, and at times, strategies that will provide you with the opportunity to experience your own epiphanies. These are the moments that will allow you to pull back the curtain of your mind, revealing the piece of the puzzle you hadn't been able to find.

You'll find this book is different than most. Unlike most books, that move cleanly from one section to the next, moving from the central theme of one chapter or idea, to the theme or core idea of the other, I have gone to great lengths to *not* arrange this book that way.

Predictability allows us to pre-judge; we anticipate the content of the next chapter or section of a book, and this all but guarantees that only a limited amount of the upcoming information will get through the screening process of our conscious mind. If you are looking for a "balanced" book, one that flows from one logical idea to the next, then this is not the book.

The structure of this book is anything but logical, everything but predictable, and guaranteed to leave you asking "Why would he have put *this* in a book on productivity?"

During the last decade I have consulted for men and women who were looking for some kind of breakthrough in their life. The thousands of hours I have spent focused like a bomb technician on the client across from me have taught me far more than I could have ever have imagined. And, while one psychologist who referred me her "difficult" clients dubbed me *The Human Whisperer™*, I have learned more from the clients I "failed" with, than the ones who were convinced I had wizard like powers and a unique insight into human behavior. All of my clients have taught me something of great value. Much of what they have taught me will be presented here; this book will share many of those lessons. Some of them very overtly, while others have been cloaked in conscious mind secrecy, leaving only your other than conscious awareness to grasp the message contained within, applying it to your unique situation, in the most appropriate and useful way.

How many epiphanies will you experience as you read *The Productivity Epiphany?* That's the best part. I can't know, and neither can you. You may have many, one right after another, or, you may only have one… initially. As the circumstances of your life change, and the frames of reference, or mental maps that you use to navigate through the world are updated, you'll find that as you return to this book from time to time, new epiphanies await, where none had existed before.

But for a moment, let's assume that you will only have one breakthrough as a result of reading *The Productivity Epiphany.* You paid less than fifteen dollars for this book. If someone you knew and trusted approached you tomorrow, tapped you with a magic wand, and gave you the experience of suddenly finding the answer to a particular challenge you had been dealing with, would you willingly pay $100, $200, or even $500 for that lone epiphany? Me too!

You may see the same concept presented more than once, in a similar, but clearly different format. When you do, it was not a mistake. We learn more than we know when we encounter the same idea more than once, from slightly different perspectives.

Reading *The Productivity Epiphany* will be like an archeological dig at a known historical site. You know that some real treasures will be found just beneath the surface; you realize you may not immediately know just what to do with some of those treasures, (or that you've even discovered a treasure until later) and you suspect that you'll meet with unexpected, but very pleasant surprises; you just don't know exactly where you'll find them. When the excavation is complete, you realize it was nothing like you thought it would be, but you realize that you have uncovered far more than you could have ever hoped for. Those treasures won't come *from* this book; they'll rise from within *you.*

I wish you many epiphanies, but whether it is one, or many, that *The Productivity Epiphany* awakens in you, I know you'll use your new awareness to take your life to a whole new level.

Chapter 1:

Effortlessly Bypassing Resistance

"One man's ways may be as good as another's, but we all like our own best."

-Jane Austen

"Look, what you need to do is just quit eating so much and start exercising!" Perhaps you have been blessed with having a concerned family member assist you with a direct suggestion such as this. Let me ask, did it motivate you? Probably not, right? In fact, you resent the person who gave you that advice, and as a result, you do just the opposite, even if what they told you would have worked for the goal you've been working so hard to achieve. Crazy isn't it? Yet, research shows that we will do things that are counterproductive and that may actually cause us harm, to "get back" at those who have hurt us in some way emotionally.

What's the solution, then, when we desire to deliver information that we wish another to act upon? By talking in a way that does not trigger the defense mechanism of the listener, we can make that information available for consideration in a way that is more easily and willingly processed. Then, if after having considered it, the listener finds it useful, they can use it in any way they deem appropriate.

I invite you to consider the experience I had several years ago. One day, while preparing for a meeting in which I would be speaking, I pulled a pair of slacks out of the closet that I had not worn for three months. I was a bit frustrated when I found the pants a little too tight around my waist. Right there and then, I said to myself, "You have start exercising more and then start eating healthier foods!" Sometimes feeling less than satisfied with your situation can serve as the launching pad for a positive action, it certainly did for me.

Now, if we look back at this last paragraph, we can see that I began by *inviting* you to *consider* something. Isn't it true, that this felt much better than the alternative of, "Listen to This!"? Next, I did not tell *you* to exercise more and eat healthier; I just told *you* what I said to *myself*. Packaged like this, you get to hear the same message of "You have to start exercising more and then eating healthier foods!" but it does not cause your "authority figure" alarm to go off, thus causing you to discount the message that may very well be useful.

I call this delivering a message under the analytical radar. Why on earth would you resist or deflect something I told you that I said to myself? You wouldn't. However, in listening to me talk about what I said to myself, you would have still heard the words "You have to start exercising more and then start eating healthier foods!" Once you have, you can comfortably decide whether or not that is something that would also benefit you. It's a sneaky way of planting a suggestion as a "seed" that, given the proper environment, can sprout into a productive behavior.

I have assisted countless people in managerial positions to speak with more precision. Initially, they are skeptical; they wonder how just a few simple changes in how they deliver their information can so effortlessly bring about the desired change. However, after they have experienced firsthand, the rapid turnaround that will result from the changes they have made, they will never again talk as they once did.

FORMULA FOR DELIVERING SUGGESTIONS UNDER THE RADAR:

1. Think about the thought, idea or suggestion you would eventually like the listener to take action on, but have the perception of it having been their idea.
2. Place the suggestion in quotes of something you said to yourself, or something that someone else said to you.

EXAMPLE:

I want someone to start getting their reports completed and turned in a little faster than they have been. So, the suggestion might be: "***Get your reports done faster than you have been or things could get ugly.***"

I might tell a story like this: "John, I'll never forget some of the lessons I learned the hard way when I first started with this company twenty years ago. There were so many little things I was doing that were causing me to have problems that were eventually going to put my job in jeopardy. We had this crotchety old manager named Bill Smith, and I'll never forget the day that he walked up to me, got right up in my face, and as he pointed his finger at me he said *'Young man, I suggest you get your reports done faster than you have been or things could get ugly!'* Can you imagine how I felt John? What do you think I did? That's right, I took his advice and my life started getting better immediately."

By hiding the suggestion in what someone else told you, you radically reduce the likelihood of John getting defensive. Because John later feels like he is doing his reports faster because he initiated the idea, you'll bypass the resentment that would otherwise occur every time John was hustling to get a report turned in a little quicker. Because he feels like it was his idea, he actually feels good about himself when he gets them completed in a timelier manner; it creates a self re-enforcing loop of success.

You'll be surprised at what you can say to other people without causing their alarms to go off. In fact, I often say to myself "You're off your rocker if you don't use the power of placing suggestions inside of quotes when talking to other people!"

As you are delivering the quote, adopt the body language and tone of voice of the person who you are describing. In the example I used, you would actually get closer to the person you are telling the story, point your finger at them, and deliver the phrase using a "Crotchety" old man voice. Doing so will feel strange the first few times, but remember, they won't be mad at you, you're just telling them what someone else said and did, and that's exactly how they'll process it consciously.

A mentor of mine perhaps said it best. He said "Use this at least five times a day for the next two weeks and you'll find that people respond to you in an entirely different way." My experience has been nothing short of what he told me.

Chapter 2:

You Better Get That Chip *on* Your Shoulder

"The authentic self is the best part of a human being. It's the part of you that already cares that is already passionate about evolution. When your authentic self miraculously awakens and becomes stronger than your ego, then you will truly begin to make a difference in this world. You will literally enter into a partnership with the creative principle."
-Andrew Cohen

When you were a child, you no doubt heard the phrase, "He's got a chip on his shoulder!" This usually had a negative connotation, referencing "his" arrogant and combative attitude. I'm going to suggest that having a "chip" on your shoulder *can* be a reason to celebrate.

Some years ago I read a fantastic little eBook called *The Self-Esteem Book,* by Dr. Joe Rubino. I can't recommend this book enough. Dr. Rubino introduces a funny looking little character named "Chip." This imaginary creature named "Chip" is introduced as the representative of our negative self-talk, and we are told that he spends his time riding on our shoulder, spewing non-sense and negativity in our ear. Furthermore, until we come to understand that "Chip" is not the "real" us, we mistake his non-sense as junk that comes from the "wise" part of ourselves. The concept of "Chip" has the ability to literally change your life. When you begin to perceive the negative self-chatter, as something that comes from outside of you, from a freaky looking entity that wants to make you feel terrible, you will make massive and immediate shifts.

Realizing how brilliant Dr. Rubino's concept was, I asked myself, "How could I make this even better, and use it in conjunction with the work I do with my clients?" If you take a moment to really think about it, when we are truly connected to what I call our "true essence", we often feel warmth, or certain sensations of pleasure in our chest and/ or abdomen. In fact, if you just take your awareness to the area around your heart, right now, you'll notice a sudden shift in your breathing, and a nice, easy, and pleasant feeling following right behind. Did you feel it? Why is this important?

Noticing that the internal garbage is not really you makes a huge difference, just by itself. However, after you immediately shift your awareness to the location of your "true essence" the effect is amplified to immeasurable degrees. After guiding clients into a deeply relaxed state, I assist them in the process of making these shifts of awareness, and thus a shift in states of mind and body, by strategically using "Chip" and the "True Essence" zone.

The moment you decide to start imagining that any negative internal chatter is coming from an evil looking little creature that rides on your shoulder, you'll finally start to grant those comments the power they deserve-NONE. Then, when you want to connect with the part of you that truly does have your best interest in mind, take your awareness to the area surrounding your heart, and as strange as it may sound, listen to what you hear when you consult your heart. You'll find great wisdom in the answers you get.

CHAPTER 3:

STOP! THERE WAS NOT A GORILLA ON THE COURT

"Focus on your potential instead of your limitations."

-Alan Loy McGinnis

Let me ask you a question; do you think you would notice a gorilla on the court during a basketball game? Not if you were doing the task that subjects at the *University of Illinois* were asked to do.

When I'm assisting someone that has been suffering with chronic pain, a question I'm often asked on the initial session is, "How is learning to think in a different way going to help my pain? My pain is real; it's not just in my mind!" To answer this, let's focus on the power of our attention, the resulting perceptions, and what role this can play in our experience of pain.

Our attention acts as a filter; a very powerful filter! In a very famous experiment on this subject, Daniel Simons and Christopher Chabris conducted a study at the *University of Illinois* that had shocking results. The subjects were asked to watch a video of a basketball game, and were tasked with just one thing; they were asked to count the number of passes made by the players wearing the white shirts.

At one point during the video, someone in a gorilla suit walked through the group playing the game, and then stood in the middle of the screen before walking slowly off the court. Over half of the subjects watching *missed* the gorilla. They simply did not see the gorilla; a gorilla that was clearly not a normal part of the context.

Our ability to notice things consciously is very limited. When the subjects had their attention riveted on the players, their brain deleted the things that didn't match what they had been asked to observe; even when those "things" were right in front of their face. Whenever I am faced with a client that has an "overactive" conscious mind that wants to "intrude" while we are doing accelerated change work, I simply utilize this principle and literally overload their conscious mind with "other" tasks. But, what about a clients ability to experience this after they go home?

A phrase that I use more and more on the initial session is "Let's get this out of the way now; I can't make you DO anything!" Many times people will say, "Can you make me stop smoking?" I respond with "Oh, believe me, I could. Sit in front of me, let me put a gun to your head, and I guarantee you will stop smoking. But that's not my line of work."

I remind them that I am a coach with some extremely impressive tools, and a great deal of skill in knowing where and when to use those tools. However, the tools that I use are only to elicit, unleash, and initiate the resources within the client. I am an active participant in a teaching process; the process of learning to use your brain to do phenomenal things. And, when my clients are good students, (and almost all clients suffering from pain are) then what can seem like magic very often occurs.

Our attention is always on something! Where we choose to place our attention will create the largest part of our reality, and, we tend to see and experience more of what we focus on, "good" or "bad". Isn't it true that the last time you bought a car, or a new dress or suit, that you almost immediately started seeing those things everywhere? They were there *before* you bought them, but the new relevancy of that car, suit or dress in your life, literally shifted your attention, thus bringing what had *always* been there into your *current* awareness.

Mastering the skill of shifting your attention can be one of the most empowering tools around. A big part of what I do is teaching people how to begin mastering this skill. I can assist people in not seeing, hearing, or feeling some things, and seeing, hearing, and feeling other things. Everyone can learn this. In fact, everyone is *already* doing it daily, just not in a way that serves them well.

So, don't be so sure that you could never miss a gorilla on the basketball court. More importantly, if this principle is at work in your life, (and it is) what "gorillas" are you missing in your daily experience because of your habitual focus of attention?

Chapter 4:

You Could Live Like a King, But Why Stoop to That Level?

"The manager has a short-range view; the leader has a long-range perspective."

-Warren Bennis

Were you aware that you have been living better than a king? I didn't know that myself for a long time, but after having come to that realization, every aspect of day to day life began to blossom with new meaning.

We make comparisons all day long. Some of those are made consciously, but for the most part this happens outside of our conscious awareness. The question is (and oh what a big question it is), what are we making our comparisons to?

Anytime you hear the words faster, better, stronger, more comfortable, or more painful, for example, you are witnessing someone who is making a comparison. They are comparing one thing to another. The challenge, however, for both you and the person speaking, is that we tend to only be conscious of one half of our comparison. We rarely think about what we are comparing something *to*.

If someone says, "I like that chair, it's beautiful!" The question is, "Compared to what?" Any time we make an evaluative statement, we have compared one thing to another thing or set of things. Yet, we don't usually say what those other things are. Again, in most cases, we simply don't know what we are using for the other side of the comparison.

Do you remember the last time you woke up, and shortly thereafter, declared the day a disaster? A "disaster" compared to what, or whom? I got up this morning and walked just a few feet to my bathroom. I then walked to the kitchen, and with the flip of a switch turned on the light, so I could open my refrigerator for something cold to drink. I plopped a couple of pieces of raisin bread into the toaster, sat down at my computer, and looked at a digital display of today's real-time weather. Oh, I forgot to mention, my rooms were dry and toasty, and I had hot water for my coffee in seconds.

I recently enjoyed another relaxing conversation with my 80 year old great aunt. The town of Trenton, Missouri had experienced about four hours with no electricity earlier in the day. Our conversation eventually led to discussing the early part of her life, and what things had been like in her younger years. Until she was married, she had never had electricity or a refrigerator in her home. Three fires were started each day to cook, even when the August heat was already pushing the inside temperature to 100 degrees Fahrenheit. Butter and milk were kept cool by placing them in a bucket and lowering them down into the well. All of this within the last eighty years!

Now, go back in time a few hundred years earlier, and pick any of the King's of that time period. Wouldn't you agree that even my great aunt, in the early part of her life, had luxuries available that the most powerful man in the land did not have a few hundred years before?

Thankfully, few of us have to deal with the conditions that she did early in life. So let me ask you, what would one of your "disaster" days seem like when compared to my aunt's everyday life in the 1930's? Almost by default, when things don't go as desired, we compare the outcome to that of one of our previous "best" days, or worse yet, to an example someone else's "best" day.

When we learn to ask ourselves, "What am I comparing it to?" and then ask this question anytime that we are feeling un-resourceful about our evaluation, our attitude will immediately begin to shift.

A study was conducted to determine why some injured athletes rehabilitate and return to their career, while others seem to crumble. Those who were successful at making the recovery, no matter how long it took, made self -to- self comparisons. In other words, they compared where they are today with where they were last week. The only thing that is important to them is the progress *they* are making.

Conversely, those that fall to the wayside get caught up in making self- to- *other* comparisons. They look at where they are compared to where one of their friends is in their current situation, and as silly as it sounds, they usually pick someone with a less serious injury! Clearly, when you compare yourself to someone stronger, prettier, taller, richer, funnier etc., you will probably wind up feeling pretty rotten. However, when you are making progress, even if it's minimal, and then noticing this progress, through your self-to-self comparisons, you will be elevating your emotions in a favorable manner.

You may be wondering if self-to-*other* comparisons are always a poor choice. Isn't it true that our society promotes self-to-other comparisons? So there must be something positive about them, right? Absolutely! The achievements of others serve as wonderful examples of what has been possible for people to accomplish. When we read and study these examples closely, we can sometimes find a blueprint for how to do it ourselves.

The danger with these "positive" examples can be found when we perceive a wide gap between what we believe this other person can do, and what we believe *we* can do. We may decide, "They must have natural talent, I could never do that!" We must always monitor our thinking to make sure that what *could* serve as a powerful motivating story, does in fact get processed in a way that motivates. If not, we run the risk of that same story "bursting our balloon" of hope and desire.

KEY IDEA:

The primary tool for achievement is measuring our own results.

When we make self-to-self comparisons, we can then look to great biographies about the achievement of others for inspiration, and not as examples to create jealousy. Below is a list of the six keys to successful athletic rehabilitation and a positive mental attitude. Please notice that these same keys can be used with great success in most any other area of life.

- Inner motivation
- The value of high standards
- Breaking goals into smaller "chunks"
- A flexible time frame
- Personal involvement/taking responsibility
- Self-to-self comparisons

You may find that reflecting on these six key areas from time to time will allow you to mentally review your life and determine where you may be off track a bit, thus allowing you to immediately take the needed action to get your "train" rolling once again.

Chapter 5:

Radio Station K-BAD MOOD

"Our appearance is a powerful communication tool, sending messages to every sighted person. Everyone is highly influenced by the visual impression of a person they are meeting for the first time."

-Catherine Bell

Have you ever found yourself in a bad mood for no apparent reason? There is a very strong possibility that it could be related to what you have been reading, or what radio station you have been listening to.

In a recent study involving our moods, John Bargh, Mark Chen, and Lara Burrows made a game that involved a scrambled sentence test. Subjects were given a scrambled sentence of fifteen words, and then had to make as many fifteen word sentences with those words as they could. One group was given words that had to do with *poor behavior,* "intrude", "aggressively" and "sarcastic." There were two other groups as well; the *neutral group* and the *polite group.* The *neutral group* was given very neutral words. The *polite group* had words such as "kind", "joyful" and "cooperative."

The subjects didn't know there were different versions of the test, and had no idea what the real purpose of the study was. Each subject had about five minutes of doing the puzzle. The crucial point came when a subject walked out of the room to inform the proctor that they had finished the test. By design, the proctor would always be talking to someone else as each person finished their test. What happened next was what the researchers were really interested in. They wanted to know one thing: would the subject interrupt? The results are very revealing.

Only15% of those who had been doing the puzzles with *polite* words interrupted within ten minutes. Those who had been using *poor behavior* word puzzles had a 60% interrupt ratio in the same ten minute period!

This technique is called the *Velten Procedure*. This method was developed in the 1960's and has unlimited possibilities for personal development. This experiment shows that by simply having someone work with certain words for a few minutes, behavior can be predictably influenced.

Our moods are heavily influenced by what we read, who we hang out with, the music we listen to, and countless other things in our daily surroundings. Unless we increase our awareness, we don't even have a say on whether or not to accept the influence. Once we are in a foul mood, everything else we encounter will be tainted with this feeling. If you "know" someone is going to be rude to you, you become rude yourself first, and then infect the other person with your mood. It's really scary how easily we push other people into roles without realizing it, and thus our own predictions are confirmed.

Listen this week to what the words of the music you listen to are "priming" your mind to think about. Do you listen to country music and songs of divorce, sadness, hangovers, and hard times? Is it possible that you could be setting your thoughts in the wrong direction each morning? What if you were to listen to upbeat instrumental music?

Have fun investigating this for yourself, and find out how many little alterations you could make that would thrust your mind in empowering new directions.

Have you ever been told, "You should never judge a book by its cover!"? Here is something you may want to consider; people DO judge a book by its cover, and more importantly, they judge you by your cover.

How many political figures do you see with facial hair? There is a reason; people tend to (on an unconscious level) distrust those with facial hair. I have found that people treat me more favorably when I my face is "clean shaved" than they do when I have a goatee. However, I want to show you something far more compelling.

Dr. Andrew Harrell, from the *University of Alberta* has shown that attractive kids are physically abused and murdered less often by their mothers than unattractive kids. Just as shocking, only 1.2% of the least attractive children were buckled in their car seats, while 13.3 %

of the attractive children were strapped in for safety. The point is clear; if physical attractiveness influences parents to treat *their own children* differently, then we cannot pretend that its power is anything less than astonishing.

The clothes we wear, the style of our hair, our posture, our voice tone, or our gestures, all help create the frame that tells others who we are. So, forget about debating whether it's fair or not. That is not relevant. The fact is, people *do* judge us by our appearance, and we all have a say in how others will perceive us, by the decisions we make about how to frame ourselves.

Take some time this week and notice how much what people wear influences the way you respond to them, it will amaze you. However, if you really want to have fun, go out of town and go into a jewelry store in your best suit or outfit. Just walk in a take note of how you are treated. Now, go back a couple of weeks later in old jeans, an old ratty T-shirt, without any makeup, and once again, notice how you are treated. If it is anything like the experiments I have conducted, you will never again doubt the power of your appearance.

CHAPTER 6:

THE MOST IMPORTANT 1/3 OF YOUR LIFE

"Crude classifications and false generalizations are the curse of organized life."
  -George Bernard Shaw

As I walked through a major pharmacy chain the other day, I stopped at the massive section of shelves that contained the seemingly endless supply of various lotions, liniments, and creams for arthritis, fibromyalgia and other types of physical pain.

Having been diagnosed with fibromyalgia in 1997, I remember all too well the constant search for the latest, greatest, miracle pain relieving product; the one that would eliminate the need for any effort on my part to improve my day to day comfort levels. I probably purchased every product that was available that promised to banish the pain from the knotted and twisted muscles in my neck, back and shoulders, between 1996 and 1998. But something happened in 1998 that would forever change my life.

In December of 1998, I completed a hypnosis certification course, at the *Hypnosis Training Institute of San Diego*, in San Diego California. I had always been fascinated with the human mind, and different forms of accelerated learning and personal development, but this was a hand's on training, with real time feedback, and experts in the area of hypnosis and NLP or Neuro-Linguistic Programming, watching and evaluating our every move.

When I initially enrolled in the hypnosis program, my goal was to simply learn more about unlocking the part of my mind that would allow me to eliminate, regulate, or modify my pain and discomfort.

One concept I learned, that I have incorporated into my protocol for pain relief, is the idea that chronic pain consists of a triad; 1/3 remembered pain, 1/3 actual pain, and 1/3 anticipated pain. Each third contributes to the overall gestalt we erroneously refer to as "constant" pain. Understandably, this model is particularly useful, as 2/3's of this gestalt do not exist outside of the life that we give them through the focus of our attention.

When one is able to banish the thoughts of yesterday's pain, and stop the frequent "replays" of past moments of pain, they will have eliminated 1/3 of the experience of their discomfort. Likewise, when a person learns how to derail the old patterns of worrying about, or anticipating how much they might hurt later today, or tomorrow, or at any other time in the future, they will have eradicated yet another 1/3 of the pain, for a total reduction of 2/3's of the previous "pain."

Before you dismiss this as nonsense, let's take a look at this from a neurological perspective that nearly everyone has experienced countless time already. Since most of us don't have a life history void of the experiences of pain or injury, we can identify with much of what we see others endure. Watching *others* in pain actually causes us to access neurological memories of the pain *we* have experienced in the past, thus bringing aspects of that discomfort into the present, even when no actual stimuli for the pain exists.

The directors of horror movies rely on this mechanism to make us scream and contort our facial expressions as we watch the poor victim on screen get a screwdriver stabbed into their eye! Did you feel that? While you've probably been fortunate enough to escape the "screwdriver in the eye" dilemma, you have most likely felt the pain of inadvertently poking yourself in the eye; you have a memory of discomforting experiences with your eye, and that's enough to cause you to squirm a little bit, just from reading about alternative uses for screwdrivers.

Several years ago, when I was in the "throes" of my fibromyalgia (a diagnosis I was given about 18 months after a serious head injury) I would wake up each day, already knowing (anticipating future pain) how bad I would feel after I got out of bed. I "knew" this because that's how I had felt yesterday (remembering past pain), and countless days prior to this particular morning. Interestingly enough, anticipating pain, and remembering past pain, both contribute in a powerful way to the present moment. In short, when we learn to experience only what is present now, and stop amplifying that experience with the misuse of the "past" and the "future" we find that we have significantly transformed our reality.

Once you have successfully eliminated the needless intrusions of the past and the future on your present moments, you can then enjoy modifying any actual discomfort of now. Fortunately, there are many effective methods available to accomplish this outcome of relief.

If you are willing to take this concept, and apply it to your own experience of pain, (physical, mental, emotional or otherwise) you will no doubt discover applications that reach far beyond the examples I've given here.

CHAPTER 7:

SAYING HELLO WITHOUT SAYING A WORD

"If you wish your merit to be known, acknowledge that of other people."
-Unknown

When we hear someone say, "He/she is an excellent communicator" we usually think of someone with strong verbal skills. While linguistic skills certainly do serve a vital role for the process of effective communication, we can quickly increase our communication and persuasion skills by learning how to consciously use communication tools that, for the most part, are unconscious behaviors.

When meeting someone for the first time, long before we are close enough to shake hands, we have the opportunity to trigger something deep inside their mind; we can trigger the part of their brain that says, "I feel good about you!"

Scientists have long known about a powerful non-verbal expression that acts as an invitation for interaction, and subtly but powerfully lets the other person know that you recognize them. The *eyebrow flash* is a behavior that is seen in every culture; whether it be tribesmen from the Amazon, or someone from one of the more sophisticated cultures on our planet, men, women and children can be observed quickly raising and lowering the eyebrows when recognizing someone they're acquainted with.

A good way to bring this more fully into your conscious awareness is to simply watch other people. More specifically, watch how people react to seeing someone they know and/or recognize. Realize that the people you are watching usually have no conscious awareness of "sending" or "receiving" the eyebrow flash, they are simply responding to this signal unconsciously.

Knowing that we automatically deliver the eyebrow flash when we see someone that we know and desire to interact with, and, how powerfully this signal impacts those we deliver it to, we can choose to use it for a different, yet extremely useful purpose.

Let me suggest that you begin using the eyebrow flash with people you don't yet know, but would like to. You'll want to use it from a distance of at least six feet, and as far away as someone can visually register the signal, like from across the room, or from the other end of an isle in a grocery store.

As you begin consciously using the eyebrow flash, you'll be delighted to notice how open people become towards you. I often walk through the grocery store eyebrow flashing anyone who happens to make eye contact with me. The result is nothing short of amazing; people smile, and I can observe them physically relaxing their posture, often initiating a conversation with me.

The eyebrow flash is very fast, consisting of a rapid rise and fall of the eyebrows, followed by a smile.

A word of warning: The eyebrow flash is such a powerful unconscious signal that unless you want to send a message of a potentially hostile interaction you should always respond to the eyebrow flash initiated by others by gently acknowledging them too.

Soon after you begin using this amazingly powerful non-verbal communication tool, you'll realize the importance of integrating this into virtually every facet of your life.

CHAPTER 8:

FORGET ABOUT BECOMING BILINGUAL; YOU BETTER BECOME TRI-LINGUAL

"Good communication is as stimulating as black coffee, and just as hard to sleep after."

-Anne Morrow Lindberg

Can you imagine showing up to a workshop or seminar, only to discover that the presenter is using a language that you don't understand? Unless you speak Mandarin Chinese, listening to a speaker using this language will be of little use in terms of learning something new. I don't know about you, but in a situation like this, I would retreat to the inner sanctuary of my mind, and engage in mental "doodling" while the nonsense took place around me, and when you're bored to tears by a speaker, I'll bet that's exactly what you do.

I'd like to talk a bit about something that's generally not thought of as a language per se, but has the power to effortlessly captivate. When ignored, it can cause other people to close their mind to any idea you present.

Each person in your audience or group has a preferred way of "listening" to the verbal world around them. Imagine for a moment that you have three different screens or filters, a screen about the size of a common house window, with a wooden paddle like handle attached.

Now, pretend that a new law requires that when listening to others who are speaking, you must choose one of the screens, pick it up by the handle, and then hold it up in front of your face. The purpose of the screen is to filter all of the words spoken by the person you are listening to. Each screen serves a different function; the first one allows only visual related words to come through. Words and phrases like "I *see* what you mean", "it was so *bright*", "the way it *gleamed*", and "the deepest *red* I had ever *seen.*"

The second one allows only the words that are associated with sounds, or auditory words like "I *hear* what you're *saying*," "*sounds* good to me" "that *rings* a *bell*" to come through.

Finally, the third screen only allows "feeling" or what's known as kinesthetic predicates and phrases through. Words and phrases like "I just need to get a *grip* on things" "It *felt* as though the sun was *warming* me right *down* to my *bones*" and "There was just a *heavy feeling* in that room."

Each person's brain has developed the cognitive equivalent of just such a screen, but rather than noticing that there are other screens available, they tend to rely very heavily on just one. Thus, their experience of the world is then "filtered" through that one conceptual screen.

Everyone has developed a particular "channel" preference; they literally feel pulled in towards you by deep feelings of intense curiosity, when you are presenting the content of your topic peppered with ample helpings of the words and phrases that originate with their "channel" preference.

I use the metaphor of "channel" intentionally. When I am in a room that has a television, I will immediately stop what I'm doing and direct my attention to the television if someone pauses on the Discovery Channel; the Discovery Channel is full of things I'm interested in, and noticing the Discovery Channel logo on the bottom of the screen says to my brain, "Hey, this is stuff you like!" Let the person with the remote flip to the cooking channel, and I'm right back to my previous project; I love to eat, and don't mind cooking, but I'm not exactly fired up when I hear others talk about it; the cooking channel is the wrong channel for capturing my attention.

When speaking to just one person, the strategy is simple; we listen for the preferred "channel" they use, and then construct our message to them, using their chosen "channel." If for example, someone said to me, "Jim called the other night and he was really *down*. I just *felt* like he needed a *lift* or something. You know, we just never know the *burden* that others are *carrying* on their *shoulders*." I would reply in their obvious "channel" preference of "feelings" or the kinesthetic mode. "Oh yes, that's *heavy* stuff. I mean, sometimes we just can't seem to *grasp* that we always have others that would *lend* a helping *hand*, and who would be glad to make our life a little *lighter*."

In the above example, the other person will feel very connected to me and the message I deliver. I could have said, "I *see* what you mean. *Look*, sometimes we just don't have a *vision* that keeps us *looking* forward, when all we really need, is to understand that there's someone out there who can *brighten* our day." With a reply like this, we might as well be from another galaxy. Neurologically speaking, it's like a foreign language.

"That's all fine and dandy Vince" you might be thinking. "But not everyone in an audience or group is going to have the same channel you bucket head, so what good will this be when I'm speaking to 25-1000 people at once, or recording an audio program that will be listened to by thousands?" My reply: "You are exactly right...you will have people with all of the channel preferences, so you have to become "tri-lingual."

As you learn to weave the words and phrases of the three major preferences into your presentations, you'll find that more and more people are leaning forward on the edge of their seats when you speak. An example of this "Tri-Lingual" approach of presenting would be, "So ladies and gentlemen, as you *envision* a future with the people around you that *support* your mission, *saying* things to yourself like 'it *feels* so good to have so many people *behind* me', you'll *see* just how good it can *feel* to have people *telling* you that you WILL make it..." Each of the three "channels" has been incorporated, and much like a buffet at a casino in Las Vegas that has been designed to have something for everyone, so too, will your presentations offer tasty morsels of verbal wisdom for your audience members.

To become masterfully proficient with this skill, think of a message you would like to deliver, and then construct it three different times, writing it out once for the visual, auditory, and kinesthetic "channels." Then, after you have reviewed the three separate messages, blend them all into one. Imagine a dark green, medium green, and a light shade of green food coloring, all three blending into the ivory white vanilla ice cream in a mixer. At first, the three shades are visible as they begin to swirl in the mixer, but within seconds, a lovely mixture has developed, and a fourth shade, consisting of all of the previous colors, but belonging to a new, and distinctly different "brand" of color will evolve.

While you won't master this skill overnight, you will be amazed at how quickly you begin to notice the use of the preferred "channel" words and phrases by others. Allow this awareness to expand each day, continually incorporating more and more of the preferred words of others into you own communication. Don't be too surprised if the knowledge of "channel" preferences finds its way into your relationships at home too. What language does your wife speak? Your children? Your husband? Your significant other? Once you know, you'll be in the position of being able to deepen those relationships. Have fun.

Chapter 9:

They Lied About Pride

"Pride attaches undue importance to the superiority of one's status in the eyes of others. And shame is fear of humiliation at one's inferior status in the estimation of others. When one sets his heart on being highly esteemed, and achieves such rating, then he is automatically involved in fear of losing his status."

-Lao-Tzu

So many of us were raised thinking that "Pride" was a good thing; we often heard things like "He's a good man, the guys got a lot of pride!" When we are seeking to build our self-esteem on a solid foundation, however, we may want to look a little closer at this "pride" creature.

Perhaps the most easily recognized sign of low self-esteem is pride. Does that shock you? Pride is a feeling that is derived from things from the outside. People who constantly profess their pride in college degrees, addresses, careers and such, are always comparing themselves to others, and looking at the things *they* have. Interestingly enough, these people usually don't think too highly of themselves.

"Is it wrong to be proud of myself?" you may ask. Of course not; listen to that question closely though. There is a big difference in being proud of *yourself* for earning the degree, and having pride *in the degree*. Simply knowing that you earned the degree and then feeling good about it is sufficient for the healthy process of feeling good about yourself. Pride, however, is not satisfied to remain quiet within; pride needs the fuel from the attention of others to stay alive.

The glue that holds pride together is that of comparison; you must compare yourself to someone you secretly know will not "measure" as high as you in the category being contrasted.

Self-esteem, on the other hand, is something that comes from within; you feel good about who you are on the inside, and feel good about your situation at any given point on your journey of achievement. The person with pride will feel good about themselves when they have finally earned their Ph.D. (they think), while the person with a strong self-esteem will feel good about themselves every step of the way. While they may look forward to the benefits of one day having their Ph.D., they are just as comfortable with themselves while working on their associate's degree, as they will be when they can finally call themselves "Doctor."

When we begin to observe the difference between pride and self-esteem in others, we'll be better equipped to see this same thing in ourselves. We will know we are operating from a healthy self-esteem when we are thinking from a mindset of abundance, aren't comparing ourselves to others and aim to give the people around us a needed boost. Saying hateful things to or about others, making comparisons to other people, and looking for our security in our outer word are all signs that we are functioning from the position of pride.

Awareness is the key that will release us from this mentally constructed jail cell of misery. Stay awake, stay the course, and watch your world change.

CHAPTER 10:

DO NOT IMITATE CUSTER'S LAST STAND

"Let no man imagine that he has no influence. Whoever he may be, and wherever he may be placed, the man who thinks becomes a light and power."

-Henry George

We all know what happened to Custer, right? It wasn't pretty. As a speaker, sales person, manager or parent, you never want to "die" in front of those you wish to influence, but if you take the wrong stand, you may very well end up "scalped" like Custer's men.

An overwhelming body of research on covert influence shows that it really does matter where we stand when we present our material. But if you're anything like me, research only serves as a good starting point...never a place to end.

To satisfy yourself that the position of your body in relationship to others is important, recruit several friends and ask them to help you out. Place two chairs face to face, just about 3-4 feet from each other. Now, assuming you are sitting in one, slide the other over about two feet to the right, so that when the other person is sitting across from you, your right eye is aligned with theirs.

Now, have each person sit across from you, evaluating on a scale from 1-10 how comfortable they are with you. After they have done so, move your chair so that they are now across from you, and on your left. Now have them evaluate again. Do this with as many people as you can find, because the results are staggering. You'll be shocked to find that almost everyone rates you as being much more comfortable when you are on their right side. The research also indicates that you will be seen as more attractive as well. Can you see how this might be beneficial?

So, how do you use this information in a live presentation when talking to a large group of people?

First of all, when you first take the stage, you'll want to stand near the center, just slightly off to the right of the audience, or your left. As the presentation moves forward, you will want to use both sides of the stage; the side to the right of the audience for anything you want them to associate positive feelings to, and the left side to the things you want them to link to negativity.

For example, if you are presenting a product or a new idea, you'll want to stand to the right of the audience when you are talking about your product or idea. Then, move carefully over to the left of the audience when you talk about your competitor.

Just in case you are wondering how powerful this is, when researchers placed goggles on test subjects that only allowed them to see off to their left, nearly all of them reported feelings of fear and panic. When the subjects wore goggles that only allowed them to look to their right, they felt an increased level of comfort and sense of calm.

Take a look at where you've been standing, and if you have been presenting from the audiences left, make sure your last presentation was the "last stand" in that position. If only Custer had known!

CHAPTER 11:

MELTING RESISTANCE WITH STORIES

"Storytellers, by the very act of telling, communicate a radical learning that changes lives and the world: telling stories is a universally accessible means through which people make meaning."

-Chris Cavanaugh

The smartest man I ever met was also the most boring. When I was in the Navy, I took a math class through *Southern Illinois University* while I was stationed in San Diego, California. This guy had worked for NASA, and could work through complex computations with blinding speed. I do good just to balance my check book, but this guy worked out problems in his head faster than the students could with scientific calculators. On top of that, he also knew a lot about everything; it didn't seem to matter what the topic of discussion happened to be, he knew something about it.

With all of this knowledge, there was one thing that prevented him from being perceived as interesting by the majority of students. All he knew how to do conversationally was convey the facts, and facts alone are boring as hell. Day after day, I watched those around me, racing each other into trance as he droned on and on. I eventually came to the conclusion that math was just one of those subjects that couldn't be fun or entertaining, and as a result, I was really struggling to grasp the concepts in a useful manner.

Years later I would meet a woman that shattered the myth that math can't be fun. Melody Shipley told stories, and these stories had embedded within them, the principles a successful math student would need. After four weeks with Melody, *at North Central Missouri College,* I had learned more than I had in the fourteen weeks with the NASA whiz bang. He told us what he knew, she told stories. He bored us to tears, and she magically captivated us all.

Captivation is the key. By capturing the attention of your audience, you can take them on a journey, traveling with them through the various feelings and emotions that support the outcome you have already decided would be beneficial for their needs. Oh, did I forget to mention that? Most people tell a story with no outcome in mind. I used to be the epitome of telling irrelevant stories that left friends and family wondering "I wonder what the point of that story was?" Several years ago, I was asked "What do you want the other person to think or feel after you tell this story?" I was embarrassed to think about how many times I had opened my trap without having any idea what the answer to that question was.

Once I learned to ask that question, it was like someone had finally greased my wheels. No longer did I feel any resistance in those I was speaking to, but instead watched as people followed me from one mood shift to the next, almost begging to be taken on the next ride through an intriguing tale. But it all started with getting their attention.

How do you do that consistently? There is one thing I have discovered that will effortlessly get people by the shirt collar, and have them glad that you did. Talk about something controversial without taking a side. For example: " Has anyone noticed how there seems to be some conflict about why our weather is changing so quickly, and whether or not this has anything to do with global warming."

Your audience will have strong feelings associated to this, and will therefore be generous with their attention. Now all you have to do is keep it. How? You ask them, "Now, what on earth could this debate have to do with why I'm here today?" You then tell them, "As I talk to you today, you'll become aware of the correlations between X and the global warming debate." As long as you provide them with something that makes a connection between the two, they'll feel the closure they need, and more importantly, what you talked about will still be in their mind tomorrow.

When I first stepped into the world of sales over 20 years ago, I chose a tough way to start. I believed then, as I do now, that a career as a door to door insurance salesman is one of the hardest selling gigs out there.

I would normally work in a community some 2-5 hours away from my home, knocking on the doors of people who had never before seen my 20 year old face, or even heard of the agency I represented in most cases. Imagine some kid that looked like they were still in high school, knocking on your door, coming in to ask you a few questions, delivering a presentation, and then asking you for $1000-$4000. Like I said, it was tough.

I was always somewhat amazed when someone got out their check book, and wrote me the check for an insurance policy they hoped was as good as I had told them. How did I do it? I 1986, I was trained, as most sales people are today, to use what Dr. Eric Knowles refers to as *Alpha Strategies*. In short, *Alpha Strategies* are techniques designed to overcome resistance. As you might imagine, there was a fair amount of resistance in those who I was asking to abandon their current insurance company, and to then trust someone who had been a total stranger less than two hours before, ultimately handing me a check for well over $1000.

The challenge we faced, as agents, was that even when we were successful at overcoming the resistance, we had done nothing with the resistance; it was still there, lurking beneath the surface, and when the emotional "high" we had induced began to wane, chances were good that the resistance would eventually prevail. To return to the home office at the end of the week, only to discover that the "Big" sale you had made had been cancelled, was like being punched right in the gut!

The world's foremost expert on resistance reduction is Dr. Eric Knowles. I've been fortunate enough to spend some time with Dr. Knowles discussing what he calls the *Omega Strategies*. It was an honor to hear the principles I had studied so thoroughly in his book resonate in the voice of Dr. Knowles himself. He presented me with several examples not contained in the book, in terms of application and use in day to day interactions.

One technique that I absolutely love, because of its simplicity and power, is that of simply acknowledging the resistance. When I first learned of this research, the part of me that was trained to sell insurance said, "Whooaaa, you're actually going to bring up the fact that they are resistant?" As a red cheeked insurance agent, I had been taught to keep them focused on thoughts that were aligned with making the decision to buy.

Knowles presents an overwhelming body of research that indicates we should in fact bring this to their attention. In one example, Knowles found that when one of his research participants asked another student, "Would you mail this letter for me?" that about 70% of those asked said yes. However, when the assistant made the same request, but first acknowledged the resistance of the person being asked, it jumped to almost 100% of the requests be answered with "Yes." What were the words that were responsible for an increase of as much as 30%? "I know you probably don't want to, but..." That's it. The question in full was, "I know you probably don't want to, but would you mail this letter for me?" How much could an increase in compliance of nearly 30% mean to you?

Knowles discovered that by acknowledging the resistance, we can lower its intensity, and in some cases, even defuse it completely.

If you have a message to deliver, and you feel you may encounter a great deal of skepticism, (resistance) tell them, "Folks, I'm going to tell you something that you probably won't want to believe,.." If you've been involved in sales or a career that requires a significant amount of persuasion for any length of time, this will initially feel like using your non-dominant hand to write with. But after you have witnessed this principle literally melt someone's resistance, you'll soon find yourself using it with ease.

Notice that when using this principle of acknowledging the resistance, the essential message has not changed or become more attractive; you have not added a "bonus" or anything else to "amp" up your offer or sweeten the request. You are simply letting the other person know, that you realize they may not want to do it, believe it or accept it.

This technique can also significantly deepen and speed up the process of establishing rapport. By acknowledging what they are feeling or thinking, it's as if you were so in tune with them that you actually read their thoughts.

One caveat: Only use this with something you are certain there is, or will be resistance to or about. Knowles found that when resistance was acknowledged, when in fact there was none, that it could have a backlash effect, and actually cause an otherwise confident person to begin to doubt what you're saying.

Remember, by first reducing the resistance to your message, you'll discover that it requires much less effort to persuade in most cases.

I remember Dr. Knowles saying, "I know this seems so straightforward and simple, that you may be hesitant to use it, perhaps even wanting to disregard it completely, but the science is there…this stuff is powerful, and will increase your persuasiveness in virtually any environment."

Having used these principles with my clients in personal coaching sessions, I can tell you that Dr. Knowles is right. You might not want to try this stuff today, but if you decide to now, I think you'll be glad you did.

CHAPTER 12:

THE POWER OF PRAISE

"A desire to be observed, considered, esteemed, praised, beloved, and admired by his fellow is one of the earliest as well as the keenest dispositions discovered in the heart of man."

-John Adams

I just love it when I'm surprised by simplicity. In a world that is racing forward with new discoveries being made daily, and technological advances in almost every field of study imaginable, it seems logical that if we just wait another week or so, we'll have access to the "be all, end all" influence technique or strategy.

What would it be like if you discovered that you already possess the knowledge and ability to do what science has proven to be the most effective concept for influencing men? Even if you work in the female oriented *Victoria's Secret*, statistics show that a significant number of purchases there are made by men. Do you think knowing what moves them to action, whether you're a man or woman, could be useful to know?

Stop for just a moment. What's the last conversation you had with someone that left you feeling good about yourself? Isn't it true that when someone has praised you, complimented you, or acknowledged you in some way, it just kind of warmed you from the inside out, made you stand a little taller, and had you smiling on the inside?

Anyone who has read Kevin Hogan's bestselling book, *The Psychology of Persuasion* (a book *everyone* should own) knows there are some incredibly powerful techniques for influencing and persuading others that have been discovered in recent years. If you have ever seen the seemingly unending rows of sales and influence books at your local book store, you'll understand why I had to pick my jaw up off of the floor when Kevin Hogan recently told me the one thing that supersedes everything else when it comes to influencing men: Praise.

That's right; your chances of influencing a man will go up exponentially when you sincerely deliver ample amounts of praise. Kevin Hogan knows more about influence and persuasion than most experts will ever forget. When he introduced me as a speaker at his famous Influence Boot Camp in Las Vegas, he said, "I've coached a few hundred public speakers in my career. Every now and then, someone comes along that makes you stop and say, 'Wow!' and I've had four or five of those people over the years. Vince Harris is one of them." Now, he wasn't using some intricate language pattern or complex persuasion strategy. Yet in that very moment, if Kevin would have been selling cheap versions of the once famous *Pet Rock*, I'd have been the first one in line.

None of us like to feel like we are being sold or persuaded; we do, however, like to feel good about ourselves. When the person that helps us do so, also happens to have a product or service available, we sure do like to "repay" them for their kind words, or, more precisely, *our* good feelings. You could actually think of it as an invisible form of reciprocity. The Law of Reciprocity states that when we give someone something that has a perceived value for them, they will feel compelled to return that favor. I ask you, what do you and I value more than a heartfelt compliment?

To be sure, there are some almost magical influence strategies that will move others to action, and they should all be used where appropriate, but they will be far more effective, when used under the canopy of praise. When you have first praised the person before you, everything else you do or say will have an amplified impact. It's easy to throw a big rock through a window, but when the window in question has already been cracked, even the smallest of pebbles will get the job done.

The next time you wish to influence someone, consider this: forget about what methods you will use, or what masterful words you might say. The words that will be heard as "masterful" by others are the ones that are used to deliver the sweet sound of praise.

You may be surprised to discover that when others feel as though you are the "angel" of good feelings, that almost any words will be effective for purpose of presenting your proposal. You'll also experience a nice shift in your own feelings when your day has been full of assisting others to feel better about *their* day.

CHAPTER 13:

THE CONSEQUENCES OF THE BRITNEY SPEARS "BUZZ" CUT

"An individual's self-concept is the core of his personality. It affects every aspect of human behavior: the ability to learn, the capacity to grow and change. A strong, positive self-image is the best possible preparation for success in life."

–Dr. Joyce Brothers

Almost everyone remembers the media blitz when Britney Spears shaved her head and let her long flowing locks fall to the salon floor. While I don't have any insight into Britney's reasoning for what was viewed by the media as a troubling indication of her instability, I can comment on how something as simple as shaving ones head can serve as the much needed spark for lasting personal change.

Few things contribute to what we will accomplish in life, or not, as much as our identity. When someone has smoked for 30 years tells me, "I haven't smoked for three months now." I'll probe a little deeper, perhaps even asking "how much longer before you smoke again?" If they tell me, "Oh, I'm a non-smoker; I was a smoker for thirty years, but I'm a non-smoker now, so never, ever again!" then I know they have made the much needed identity shift that will all but guarantee their continued success. It's one thing to stop a behavior; it's an entirely different "animal" though, when you change "who" you are, and how you perceive yourself.

Behind nearly every lasting change, upon closer examination you'll find an identity shift that serves as the glue that holds the transformation together. Very few people have the tenacity required to maintain behavioral changes made without the rock solid foundation offered by a change in identity.

Have you ever wondered why new inductees in the armed forces have their heads shaved? It's really very simple; a person's chosen hair style has literally been "fused" with their identity. This is why women who lose their hair while undergoing chemotherapy often describe the hair loss as the worst part of the treatment. This also explains why millions of men spend more on products promising to grow hair each month than they put into their retirement account.

When the Army shears the young recruits like so many sheep in the spring, they have taken a crucial step in reshaping how these young men and women see themselves; when there are no longer individual hairstyles, and everyone looks the same, an identity "vacuum" is created. It's much easier for the Army to install the beliefs needed to make an obedient soldier when they don't have to wrestle with an identity that may or may not be "accepting" of the new values and guiding principles offered by the military.

As strange as it sounds at first, if your goal is to lose weight for example, rather than focusing on forcing yourself to eat less and exercise more, you may want to first "become" the kind of person who eats only healthy foods and who can't imagine a day ending before you've exercised. When you begin by first adopting the identity of a person who easily and naturally eats well and exercises daily, you'll find that doing those things will soon seem like second nature.

How do you do that? We can learn a great deal by looking at award winning actors like one of my favorites, Robert DeNiro. When preparing for a role in an upcoming film, actors and actresses will step completely into the character they will be portraying. In fact, some of them "become" their character so fully, that they often have difficulties "breaking character" and require rather intense debriefings to get back to "themselves" once the film has been finished. What would happen if they kept up this "pretending" indefinitely? The time would arrive, when they would find they had crossed the point of no return; they'd no longer identify with many of the beliefs and values that had served as their guide posts for most of their life.

With a new identity comes new patterns of thinking, new patterns of behaving, and ultimately new and different results. Will the changes that result from Britney having shaved her head be in her best interest? We can only wait and see. One thing is certain though, with such a radical shift in her "look" she'll no doubt experience new thoughts, new feelings, and in the end, new behaviors.

One final thought. If you find yourself a bit unsettled by the word "pretending" as a way of changing your identity, I invite you to consider the following. At some point in your youth, perhaps at some early point in school, you were accepted into a certain social group. It might have been the "Jocks", the "Geeks" or some other group that you found comfort being a member of. There were certain things the "cool" people in those groups did and said, and because you wanted to be accepted by the others, you too, started to do those things. At first you were pretending, but eventually, you were no longer making the conscious choice to behave that way; the behaviors had become habitual unconscious behaviors.

What would happen if you pretended that you were a consistent investor for a year? What would happen if you pretended you were a wonderful public speaker for eighteen months? Isn't it true, that there's a part of you that can already sense the answer to those questions? Follow that inner voice, and build the identity that will support the achievement of any worthwhile goal.

CHAPTER 14:

LESSONS FROM THE HARDY WOMEN OF THE NORTH

"In order to succeed, people need a sense of self-efficacy, struggle together with resilience, to meet the inevitable obstacles and inequities of life."

-Albert Bandura

There are few things that affect the quality of our lives as much as our ability to bounce back after getting "knocked down."

If there is one thing in this life I know to be true, and that science continues to find new support for each year, it's that we can alter our response to "stressful" events and situations, thus improving our quality of life.

A study at the *University of Alberta* shows us, once again, that we have reason to celebrate our ability to change. Dr. Beverly Leipert decided to study a group of women who have always had it "tough." She chose to conduct a study on resilience, studying women who had spent their lives living separated from others, enduring month after month of brutal cold; the women of the frozen North.

Each of the women in Dr. Leipert's study had lived much of their lives in the rugged terrain of Northern British Columbia. These women had lived with a rather unique set of risk factors; the bitter cold, attitudes regarding gender, threats posed by local wildlife, and very limited resources. These were not sporadic risks, they were simply a way of life, and were present each day.

After Dr. Leipert had compiled her findings, she discovered the three main strategies that were responsible for their resilience: 1. Becoming what she called "hardy." 2. Making favorable meanings or "stories" about their situation in the North. 3. Supplementing what the

North had to offer.

Each of these women had learned to become self- reliant, had followed various spiritual or religious beliefs, had developed a liking for the outdoor activities like camping, fishing and skiing, learned indoor activities like painting, sculpture, or quilting, and had decided to volunteer for community groups and activities.

Notice that each of the actions or behaviors above were *learned*, or *chosen*. The resilience they had developed was not some genetic gift or spontaneous phenomenon; they had taken active roles in creating the experience of the life they were living, and the level of resilience they had developed.

I'm often asked what I think about the role of DNA, or our genetic makeup, and a propensity to have certain "strengths" and "weaknesses." Make no doubt about it; there can't *not* be a genetic role in our lives. Just being alive is genetic. However, because at this point and time, there is very little we can do to alter our genetic makeup, I've chosen to focus on the parts of our experience that we *can* influence.

What can we learn from these hardy women of Northern British Columbia? First, we can accept, or not, that the quality of our lives will involve taking responsibility. When I work one on one with clients who desire to make a change in their lives, I use leading edge tools and strategies to assist them in doing so. As powerful as some of these tools are though, unless I successfully convey one thing in particular to each client before we begin, the tools will be useless: Each Client Is Expected To Work Hard. The legendary Green Bay Packers coach, Vince Lombardi was a brilliant coach to be sure, but were it not for the football players that were as dedicated to carrying out the tasks he assigned, as he was to creating them, the world would have never heard of Vince Lombardi.

Know that "bad" stuff is going to happen. The question is this, are you comfortable with the way you have reacted to the "bad" stuff that has happened in your past?

We can stop reacting and start responding the moment we decide to take an active role in how we will interact with life in the future. To bury our head in the sand and hope that nothing else "bad" happens is not only ineffective, it's downright deceptive and dangerous.

Think about a pin ball machine. Decide today to stop being the "ball", and make the decision to become the "flipper." The ball is at the mercy of everything else around it, but the flipper, now that's a different story. While the flipper cannot control 100% of what happens inside that machine, *it can influence the outcome* to varying degrees. How do we alter these "varying degrees" in our favor? Let me illustrate.

When I was in high school back in the early 80's, we had a local arcade with all of the popular video games of that era. There was a kid that had his name in the number one position on just about every game in the building. Was John the recipient of some special genetic code for arcade game mastery? No, John was a "master" for one very good reason; any time of day you walked into the arcade, John was playing and getting better. John could smoke me on any arcade game because he had played more; he practiced every day of his life, and had therefore refined his arcade game skills.

Realize that once you decide to become the "flipper" in your life that you might "tilt" a few times at first, but like any skill in life, you'll get better the more you "play."

Look back through this chapter and take some time to discover how you can apply the three main strategies used by the Northern women to your own life. Just remember, whoever said that old dogs can't learn new tricks, was probably a pathetic trainer with *young dogs* as well. No matter how you have reacted in the past, know that you can learn to respond in new and more useful ways.

CHAPTER 15:

WHAT IF EVERYONE WERE NAKED?

"Leadership is an opportunity to serve. It is not a trumpet call to self-importance."

-J. Donald Walters

Being naked is the great status equalizer. Think about the last time you got on an elevator; no one talked, but everyone was making snap judgments about others, by looking at the clothes and jewelry they were wearing, and items they were carrying.

Some might have had well pressed and very expensive suits, others may have been wearing elegant diamonds, or carrying very pricey lap top computers. Perhaps someone was wearing a work shirt with their name across the pocket, with well worn work boots, and a tool pouch hanging from their belt.

Imagine for a moment that the next time you got on an elevator everyone was naked. There were no uniforms or suits by which to classify others; there was no jewelry or laptops, or tool pouches, nothing at all, just people-naked people.

Do you realize how helpless you would be? We all have a deep and curious nature that likes to place others into a "box." When we have discovered "who" someone is, we can conveniently place our label on them and never have to "think" again.

While this strategy sure makes it easy for us, (in terms of mental energy) we have to realize that this is the same strategy others use to "figure us out." This has a lot to do with why you can never be a hero in your own home town.

When a company sends someone to pick me up at the airport for a speaking engagement, this person sees me coming off the plane looking very sharp, already knowing that I will be paid several thousand dollars for presenting that day. They have "figured me out" and have decided that I'm someone "important."

However, when I go into the local grocery store in my hometown, it doesn't matter that I travel the world, speaking to powerful men and women; to those who have known me since I was a little boy, I'm still the skinny little kid who could be seen pushing his lawnmower through town, mowing yards and raking leaves. The skinny little kid is "who I am" to them, and the speaking and traveling is "what I do."

But let's get beyond being naked; let's look at the fact that we are much more than our physical bodies.

You have an arm, but you're not your arm. You have eyes, but you're not your eyes. You have legs, but you're not those legs. Even organs; you have kidneys, but you're not those kidneys. People can live for long periods of time having their blood filtered by a machine-without having kidneys. Many people are walking around with some else's heart, or liver, or eyes.

What, and who are we then? I'm comfortable telling you that I have not a clue; I am even more comfortable telling you that I know we are much more than we think we are. Because we can all begin to sense this "truth" when we are open to it, we can also begin to make contact with, and live more fully from this "part" that comes to this awareness.

Kind of confusing isn't it? One thing I like about it, though, is that it can be as spiritual or religious as we want it to be, or it can be as scientific and tangible as we'd like to think. The only thing that really matters is that you know you can acknowledge the fact you are more than your physical body.

This has proven to be a useful concept for those who had been suffering with chronic pain. I teach them how to dis-identify with their physical body, realizing that while they might "have" an arm that is experiencing pain, they are not their arm, and therefore, neither are they the pain they can notice in that arm. I'm confident, that given enough time, your mind will generate many useful applications of this idea into your life too.

CHAPTER 16:

GET TO BED EARLY AND BEHAVE MORE ETHICALLY

"A man's ethical behavior should be based effectually on sympathy; education, and social ties: no religious basis is necessary. Man would indeed be in a poor way if he had to be restrained by fear of punishment and hope of reward after death."

-Albert Eintsein

Unless you've been vacationing on another planet for the last 20 years, you are very much aware of the importance of sleep for optimal health. Recent findings are shedding new light on this favorite nocturnal activity, however.

Three years ago, while out walking my dog one evening, a good friend of mine's father pulled over to the curb to visit. He had just come home from the hospital after a coronary bypass surgery, and was out for a leisurely drive. "It was a hell of a deal." Bill snapped. "The Dr. told me we needed to get it done right away, and that it was up to me, but we could do it that night if I wanted."

Bill continued, "I looked him square in the eye, and said "Doc, if it's all the same to you, I think I'd rather have you 'cuttin' on me when you're fresh. Go ahead and schedule me for the first patient on a morning after you've had a good night's sleep!"

Bill's common sense approach to open heart surgery isn't necessarily shared by the rest of the world.

Living in the high consumption society that we do, we often find ourselves dealing with people who are trying to function after getting much less sleep than their body needed.

To be able to meet the demands of a world that says, " But I want it NOW!" everyone from the banker to the undertaker has had to extend their hours of business, thereby leaving only one option for those who want to maintain the time spent with loved ones, hobbies, and other activities: Sleep less. This willful act of "burning the candle at both ends" comes with consequences though; and it turns out that the consequences reach further than previously thought.

In a study at the *Walter Reed Army Institute of Research*, they discovered that sleep deprivation leads to a rapid and significant decline in our ability to act in accordance with our moral beliefs.

William Killgore, Ph.D. revealed that the results of the study suggest that when sleep deprived, individuals appear to be selectively slower in their deliberations about moral personal dilemmas relative to other types of dilemmas." Is there some context in your life that you've been making poorer choices than what you're capable of?

While experts recommend we all get 7-8 hours of sleep a night, only you know what it takes for you to operate in your peak performance zone. For some it may be as little as four hours, while others may be "ragged" after anything less than nine.

How much more effective would you be as a parent if you were always fully rested? As a teacher? Coach? Employee? Employer?

Like it or not, we come up against moral "dilemmas" almost every day. The quality of our lives ultimately boils down to the quality of our decisions, and the quality of our decisions can be traced to our mental and emotional states.

Getting the sleep you need is perhaps the easiest way to support your mental and emotional states. And, the other people in your life will most likely appreciate your new found pleasant demeanor and ability to live in accordance with your values.

CHAPTER 17:

YOU MEAN THE NAZI'S WEREN'T EVIL DEMONS?

"She was beginning to understand that evil is not absolute, and that good is often an occasion more than a condition."

-Gilbert Parker

I'll never forget a conversation I had about a year ago regarding the Nazi Death camps of World War II. An older gentleman was out for his afternoon coffee, and was seated just a few feet from me in the Hy-Vee Deli, a local grocery store in Trenton, Missouri.

After a segment on the Holocaust had just finished on the television in the deli, he growled, "That was some hellacious and unthinkable stuff those damn Germans did to the Jews!" "I won't argue with that; it's hard to imagine that many people being murdered in such a short time." I replied.

The old man shot back, "It's an evil human being, no, the brother of the devil himself, that could do such a thing." No doubt expecting me to agree with him, he stiffened as he listened to my comeback.

"Not as evil as you think." I said. "I'm guessing there are 100 people shopping in this store at the moment, and I'm betting that under similar circumstances, at least 50% of them would have followed the orders to do the very same reprehensible acts that the German soldiers did!"

"You must be out of your friggen mind!" he said in a loud voice. I calmly said "One would like to think so, wouldn't they? Unfortunately, though, there's a pile of research, and some landmark studies that say otherwise."

Over the next 30 minutes, I gently and carefully presented the information that I had based my comments on, and interestingly enough, he was not only becoming calmer, but instead scratched his head saying, "I'll be damned kid, who would have guessed?

Are you wondering what I could have possibly said to not only defuse the anger this man was rapidly starting to generate, but that actually opened his mind enough to get him to consider the possibility, that it really doesn't take a black hearted human being like Jeffery Dahmer to be able do such horrible things to others? Here it comes.

In 1963, Stanley Milgrim stood the field of psychology on its head. In this famous study, Milgrim wanted to observe the tendency of people to obey authority figures. Milgrim was troubled by how quickly the German citizens had followed the orders of Adolf Hitler, to do things like brutally slaughter millions of Jews.

Milgrim's study involved telling the participants that they would be assisting him in studying the effects of learning; more specifically, the effects of punishment on learning.

At the lab, they drew pieces of paper to see who would be the "teacher" and who would be the "learner." Little did they know that it was rigged so that they would all be in the role of "teacher."

The "learner" (who was secretly working with Milgrim, and posed as a student) would be strapped into a chair that could deliver shocks when they made a mistake on the test. They would be seated in another room, out of view from the "teachers" but close enough they could be heard. The "electric chair", while looking very real, could not deliver a shock at all...it was all a set up.

Soon after the "learning experiment" had begun, the "learners" started making mistakes (as they had secretly been instructed to) on the test they were taking. Each time a mistake was made, the researcher would instruct the "teacher" to administer a shock. Although the "voltage" used started out at rather harmless levels, after just a few mistakes the "voltage" had been dialed up to 300 volts. At this intensity, the "learners" were yelling in anger and pounding on the walls. (Again, keep in mind, they were acting. They weren't being shocked at all, but the "teachers" didn't know that.)

It was at this point that the "teachers" would begin looking to the research person for guidance. Yet, when they did, they were simply asked to deliver yet another shock, but at a higher "voltage." Each time they would seek advice or support, the researcher firmly suggested that they go ahead and give a more powerful shock to the "learner."

By the time each "teacher" was told to stop, the "voltage" administered had gone all the way up to 450 volts. This is a voltage that, had it been real, clearly had the potential to kill the "learners." At "450 volts" the "learners" were screaming bloody murder, and begging for their lives.

This is where it becomes mind blowing. Twenty six of the forty "teachers" in the study delivered all 30 levels of shock! Many of those who delivered all 30 shocks felt a great deal of distress *about* what they were doing-but they did it anyway. Stanley Milgrim had discovered that the power of authority was far more influential than he could have ever suspected.

Were those who delivered the "painful" shocks to those who were begging for mercy social outcasts and degenerates? Far from it. They were students. These were people who were on the honor roll, or were rated as being very likable and generous citizens.

Just in case you're wondering, yes, this study has been repeated numerous times, and the results were always the same.

How do we explain such behavior? Milgrim concluded that when others are given instruction by a perceived authority figure, it can make very normal and decent people do very *abnormal* and horrible things. He further concluded that evil actions do not necessarily have to come from an evil person.

Finally, and perhaps most frightening, Milgrim concluded that under the right circumstances, and in the right situation, any of us might obey orders to maim, injure, or even kill another human being.

Do you think the some 900 people the Rev. Jim Jones ordered to drink poisoned Kool-Aid were just stupid? Not a chance. The Law of Authority was alive and well in Guyana in 1978. When I was just twelve years old, I watched as the evening news showed the overhead photos of hundreds of bloated bodies stacked upon one another. The news anchor said that preliminary reports suggested that they may have willingly poisoned themselves. That was just too much for my young mind to comprehend. "Why on earth would you do what someone told you, if you knew it was going to kill you?" I wondered.

Do you think your kids are smart enough to not take drugs when a stranger offers them? Let's hope so. However, it's not strangers we have to worry about. See, when my parents warned me about the "bad" things in life, I always had this image of some surly and ragged looking bum, someone I could clearly see as someone I shouldn't trust, as being the kind of person that would eventually offer me psychedelic mushrooms, so I could take a "magic carpet ride."

But that's not how it happens, is it? No, the "bum" often turns out to be a trusted friend, or someone we have known for some time. Worse yet, it may be someone who we see as an authority figure. For a freshman in high school, a senior on the football team may be viewed as an authority figure for some kids; it doesn't have to be a middle aged man with a badge for the Law of Authority to prevail.

In conclusion, it does not require an evil person, to do an evil thing. All it takes is the right combination of environment and people. It may also be wise to familiarize yourself and your family with this phenomenon. Teaching your children to always obey their elders, may not be the best advice you can give.

Chapter 18:

Nothing You Fear Losing Can be the True Source of Your Happiness

"As human beings we all want to be happy and free form misery…we have learned that the key to happiness is inner peace. The greatest obstacles to inner peace are disturbing emotions such as anger, attachment, fear and suspicion, while love and compassion and a sense of universal responsibility are the sources of peace and happiness."

-Dali Lama

One of the "secrets" of happiness can be found in the following question:

What would you want if you didn't have to be unhappy about not getting it?

Let me explain a little further. Millions of people each day settle for far less than what they are capable of, for one simple reason; they are afraid of how they would feel if they tried, but failed. Ahhh, there's that loathsome word-failure.

It has been written about in hundreds of wonderful little books, and my personal experience has confirmed the following concept: We learn very little when we succeed at something, but have the potential to learn loads of valuable stuff when we fail.

Please notice that I said "potential" to learn. If, as was common to me in my very rebellious teens and twenties, we become angry and/ or dejected by failure, and instead of gathering all the useful data and charging back into the game, we say " screw it!" and give up or quit, then that potential has been wasted.

What a delightful surprise it is, though, to discover that as we remain calm and collected, the pieces of the puzzle begin to fall into place, and our failure becomes the very thing we needed to be able to progress to the next step.

Here is yet another way of looking at the secret being revealed in this chapter:

Nothing we fear losing can be the true source of our happiness.

"But wait a minute" you may scream. "I fear losing my children, and they make me happy!" If this thought popped into your head, believe me, you're not alone. This was the very thought that had me hung up…for about fifteen minutes.

Let me ask you, have you ever known, or heard about someone, that even though they may have suffered the loss of a child, or in the worst case scenario, all of their children to some tragedy, in spite of their pain and anguish, they have gone on to live many vibrant and quality years, truly feeling happy? Do you think the world is full of people like this? Just in case you don't know for sure, the answer is a resounding "YES!"

TRY THIS ONE ON FOR SIZE:

The only reason you are ever unhappy is because you think you should be.

When you feel "bad" it's for one of two basic reasons:

1. You think that is how you are supposed to feel at that moment.
2. You don't know how to change how you are feeling at that moment.

Behind every justification someone has for feeling bad, there is almost always an un-resourceful belief holding those thoughts and feelings in place.

I was once working with a lady who had been experiencing a very prolonged grieving period from the loss of her spouse. It had been just over a year and a half since her husband had died, and she was still weeping and moping around, not ever really having stepped back into "life."

On our second session together, I asked her, "What would it mean about you, if you were no longer miserable, and actually started to enjoy life once again?"

As she sat there processing that question, I watched as her face literally began to contort and change, as her emotional landscape rapidly shifted from one feeling to another.

Suddenly, she drew a long deep breath, and began to cry, while breaking into the most beautiful smile I've ever seen on a client. "It would mean that I don't love him anymore." She said softly, having just come to the realization that this faulty unconscious belief had been driving her behavior and emotions for nearly two years.

That was the "hard" part; making the unconscious something that she was now conscious of. Only then could it be worked with and modified. In her case, however, just having the belief or thought out in the open where she could observe it, had already started to weaken it considerably.

The rest of our time was spent deconstructing that belief completely, and then "placing" a more useful belief in its place.

As long as she felt like she had a good reason for feeling unhappy, even if she felt this on an unconscious level, it was highly unlikely that she would have interrupted this pattern that had upset the normal structure of her life, and thus, her happiness.

If you find that you've been far too unhappy about something lately, or have felt a sense of continuous and ongoing unhappiness about something, perhaps it's time to ask yourself, "What would it mean about me if I was no longer unhappy about this?"

The answer may be immediately available, or it may require your patience as you simply wait for it to arrive. The important thing is that after you have your answer or answers, you place them under the "microscope", scrutinizing them to see if they still "make sense."

The same belief that had reached a point of no longer making sense for my client would have made perfect sense for a short period of time after her husband's death. Beliefs are to be used as guidelines, not truths. We need to occasionally run checks on the "guidelines" we are using, and when we find one that's out of date, we need to toss it like the milk that has soured, and pick up a fresh one that we can use.

CHAPTER 19:

How Becoming More Productive is Like Brushing Your Teeth

"If you create an act, you create a habit. If you create a habit, you create a character. If you create a character, you create a destiny."

-Andre Maurois

About a year ago, while settling into my seat on my flight out of San Diego, I pulled John Maxwell's book, *Today Matters: 12 Practices to Guarantee Tomorrow's Success* from my brief case, and opened it to the page I had folded down a few hours before. As I began reading, the words warmed me from inside; something I have come to expect when I read the works of John Maxwell. Suddenly, my mind screamed "Go back read that again!" I quickly back tracked to re-read the passage. John was right.

We can't significantly change our life until we are willing to change something we do every day

Just as I started to feel the impact of this penetrating my very being, I was interrupted by the woman sitting next to me, "Could you keep an eye on this?" she asked as she handed me the book she was reading. I jumped right back into my book. John's words were reverberating through my mind.

How many times have you read or heard "3-5 days of exercise a week will yield great benefits to your health"? They're right; 3-5 days will yield wonderful results for most people, but there's a problem built into the solution in this case.

When we begin something that has an immediate and intense "payoff", at least in terms of how it makes us feel, we are inclined to slowly, and sometimes instantly increase the frequency of that behavior. The sudden rush that someone feels from cocaine, for example, will quickly take a three time a week user, to an everyday user.

However, when we begin something that not only lacks an immediate "good" feeling, but that may very well result in some initial discomfort, then the pendulum swings the other way for a time. The four day a week early morning walk, becomes a three day a week morning walk, and then two, one, and eventually, you're saying "I really need to start exercising again."

Let me ask you, when was the last time you said "I really need to get back into brushing my teeth"? Or, when was the last time you were running so late for work or an appointment, that you decided to just skip brushing your teeth? I'm guessing you said "Never!" to both of those questions. Because we were taught to brush them every day, and were forced to do so, it was neurologically "wired in" becoming a habit that was resistant to change. It's simply not conceivable to think of *not* brushing our teeth every day.

When we do something periodically, we're sending our nervous system conflicting signals. One day we send the message of, "Get used to this walk at 6:00 am each morning" and the next day we send the message of "Okay nervous system, get used to sleeping in until 8:30 am every morning." Back and forth, back and forth, back and forth. We make it almost impossible, very difficult at best, for our nervous system to "wire" the behavior in as a constant and permanent behavior, like it did with the act of brushing our teeth.

So, how do we use this knowledge? I have to admit, nearly a decade ago now, I used to sell the idea of developing the habit of walking or exercising 4-5 times a week to the clients I worked with on health issues. Shame on me! For all the magic I was able to assist my clients to create in their lives, I had fallen short of excellence regarding the development of deeply etched habitual behaviors. I'm happy to say that for some time now, my clients have learned a much different philosophy.

Do you need to start exercising, but have allowed yourself to get grossly out of shape? Then start walking, every single day, even if you have to start with 1- 3 minutes a day. How surprised will you be to discover, that after only ninety days of performing a behavior, back to back, day in and day out, that you have developed a habit that is as resistant to change as brushing your teeth?

The more you do something, the easier it becomes to do the next time, that is, as long as not more than 24 hours elapses between this time and the last. As you begin to use the "everyday" philosophy to start creating rock solid habits in your life, you'll find that the more you experience the changes that improve the quality of your life, the more you'll employ this incredibly simple strategy.

Where can you start today? You might find it beneficial to choose one of the following as the first behavior to embed into your unconscious and automatic behaviors:

- Spending fifteen solid minutes of communicating with your spouse or child each evening, maintaining direct eye contact the entire time.

- Deep breathing with your eyes closed for thirty seconds before each meal.

- Walking or exercising every day.

It's rather exciting, is it not? Think of it; you can decide on any behavior you'd like to have as a way of life, and make it so! Forget about waiting until you feel like it. If it's not already a habit you desire, chances are you'll never "feel like it." Utilize the power of acceptance to neutralize any initial resistance you might experience.

Instead of making a miserable attempt at ignoring or denying your initial resistance to engaging in the new behavior each day, (which only makes it worse, by the way) embrace the resistance with open arms, and engulf the resistance with an attitude of acceptance, and watch what happens. Why shouldn't you enjoy the experience of melting your resistance away with an attitude of acceptance?

CHAPTER 20:

YOU PROBABLY WON'T BELIEVE THIS, BUT...

"Our age is bent on trying to make the barren tree of skepticism fruitful by tying the fruits of truth on its branches."

-Albert Schweitzer

Rare is the man or woman that doesn't find themselves having to communicate on a frequent basis, with someone who seems to argue or refute almost anything they say. It may be a spirited child or student, a spouse or significant other, or an employee or employer. The fact of the matter is, some people are compelled to resist, and I know, because I'm a reformed "resister."

Researchers are finally starting to ferret out some important data, shedding new light on the topic of these knee jerk reactions or "resisting." Some of this research indicates that these unruly reactions may very well have a genetic basis. My own experience long ago validated, that, somehow, my own DNA was involved in my unexplained rebellion.

I can still remember coming home from school, thinking about all of the things I was going to tell my parents about the day, and as excited as I may have been, the moment one of them said, "What did you do at school today?" I was compelled to clam up; it literally felt like I was being interrogated, even though they had simply asked about my day. When this occurred, I felt like I split into two different people. Part of me was hell bent for leather, refusing to budge and give in, while another part of me was deeply saddened by the fact that I really wanted to share my day at school with them, but that I just couldn't let myself.

Recent studies have shown that some people are "wired", neurologically, in a way that makes their sensitivity to perceived stress much higher than for most. Notice, I said "perceived" stress, because it's all about perception. What seems like a harrowing experience for one person, may simply be the juice that makes life shine with passion for another. You might think of it like this. To the person that always resists the information you present them with, any information that comes their way is viewed as an intruder of sorts. They experience a stress response, even to information that would be non-stressful to others.

When we begin to realize that these people will usually feel the need to refute and resist, we can design our communication in a way that respects this inner need of the other person, fulfilling their desire to counter our proposal or request, while simultaneously creating the environment that is conducive for the response we desire.

The world's foremost expert on resistance reduction is *University of Arkansas* Psychology Professor, Dr. Eric Knowles. Dr. Knowles has outlined several methods that have proven to be extremely effective for reducing resistance in others, with one of them being almost embarrassingly simple.

Knowles and his colleagues discovered that by simply acknowledging the resistance in others, we can bring about a significant decrease in how deeply they have dug their heels into the dirt if you will. In one study, Knowles found that when they stopped someone and asked, "Would you mail this letter for me?" that roughly 70% complied. They experienced an immediate increase of 30% by simply inserting a short phrase just before the request. When they began by saying, "I know you might not want to…" And then followed with "would you mail this letter for me?" 100% of those asked said yes.

In my work with the clients that have hired me as their personal coach, both face to face, and over the telephone, I have found the work of Dr. Knowles to be very instrumental in the results my clients achieve. I only wish I would have known this information years ago.

I'll share with you some of the ways I've incorporated this concept into my communication with those who have come to me, more often than not, because they have recognized the resistance they have to their own desires and wishes. I must tell you, though, it took me several years to understand that even though someone had willingly come to me because they wanted to make a particular change, that they would often times be just as resistant to me, as they had been to their own attempts to change a behavior. The fact that someone would pay a considerably amount of money, only to fight the very change they were paying for was unthinkable to me, perhaps because I wasn't sure how to effectively work with their illogical behavior.

Once I have established that the client I'm working with is resisting most of what I say or present, I'll switch into a different mode of operation. I might say, "John, you're probably going to think that what I'm going to tell you is crazy, and will think that it won't work, but I'm going to throw it out there anyway, just to see what you think."

If John has previously demonstrated that his mind darts in the opposite direction, then John will be compelled to refute and disagree with what I have just told him. In fact, my experience has been that John will most likely say something like "No, no, no, I won't think its crazy, or that it won't work-go ahead, I'm listening."

When this happens, John has been given the satisfaction of resisting what I told him, and, when he then agrees with the suggestion that follows, he'll also have earned the right to thumb his nose at me, thinking, "See, I told you so. You thought I was going to tell you that was crazy and wouldn't work."

By giving the client the opportunity to respond in a way that he is neurologically inclined to do, I have then opened the gate of his mind, which then embraces my suggestion and allows it to impact his or her thinking and behaving. In its entirety, it might look something like this. "John, you're probably going to think that what I'm going to tell you is crazy, and will think that it won't work, but I'm going to throw it out there anyway, just to see what you think. John, you could really benefit from eating only fruit until noon each day."

Another method I have found to be almost magical in its ability to coax others into accepting a suggestion is that of extending an invitation to find the weaknesses in my proposed ideas. "John, I know you'll most likely find this idea to be full of holes, but I'm going to stick it out there anyway, and ask that you analyze it carefully, noting the parts that won't work." Again, my experience has been that the client will most often swat away or refute my suggestion that they find the problems of my idea, and then become open to the idea itself. In the event that the client does resist some or all of the idea, it is usually a much "softer" version of rejection, and keeps the level of rapport between us that had been previously established.

I'm certain that you'll find what I'm about to tell you a bit off the wall and not worthy of pursuing, but I'll tell you nonetheless; if you will use this information for the next 30 days with people who have routinely resisted your ideas, you'll never again be without these magnificent communication tools as you seek to influence others.

CHAPTER 21:

We are Equal as Far as Worth Is Concerned- And that's About It

"As we grow as unique persons, we learn to respect the uniqueness of others."
-Robert H. Schuller

We often hear parents say, "The most important thing I can give my children is my love." While this warms your heart, initially, upon further investigation, it may not be as reassuring as we first thought. Things are done to children by parent's everyday under the guise of "love"; things that do little to bolster the self-esteem of these children, and in many cases, literally undermine the child's sense of self. "Honey, you should be playing football, not fooling with this art. The reason I'm not going to let you sit in your room and work on these crazy oil paintings is because I love you." When a parent tells their teenage son or daughter some far-fetched tale like this, it's a clear example of how little they know about human nature.

Why, then, as parents, do people continue to say and do things like this? The manner in which we parent is most often the result of the cumulative effect of many generations before us. Were you ever spanked and told "I'm only doing this because I love you"? Is it any wonder, then, that many men grow into big husky adults who knock their wives around, truly believing that their actions are warranted and sincerely born from feelings of love?

The comeback to this by many is often "Yes, but there's a BIG difference between the mind of a child, and that of an adult; adults should know better!" It's been once said that you can tell more about a person by watching them for thirty seconds under stressful conditions, than by a lifetime of observation under relaxed conditions. My experience tells me this is true, in most cases. I've not yet met a man or woman that when placed under a sufficient amount of stress, doesn't revert to some very childlike and/or irrational behavior.

You've probably read about a respected politician or Hollywood star that has shot holes in their wife's car, or burned their husband's house down during a volatile divorce. When we are operating from deep emotional programs, logic is often lost in the shuffle. Although it's a generalization, with clear exceptions, those that had their self-esteem nurtured as children, will function more effectively under stress as adults.

How do we make sense of this? Dr. Steven Reiss, a psychology professor at *Ohio State University*, discovered that there are sixteen basic desires that drive human behavior. Each of us has our own distinct profile. For each of the 16 desires, we will find we are driven powerfully, moderately, or not much at all-or somewhere in between.

For example, the desire for *social contact* is very powerful for some. Many attend a different organization or club meeting each night of the week, and love it. On the other hand, someone else may rate that desire very low, craving a great deal of privacy and doing things at home with only family members.

Reiss points out that the strength of our desires is usually formed very early in life, and while they can change as we age, our overall profile will remain much the same. Why is this important? If you have a teenager with a low desire for *physical activity*, and a high desire for *independence*, and you're trying to force them into playing football in high school, you risk damaging the relationship with the child, and fueling the fire of resentment, neither of which will do much for their self-concept or self-esteem.

If you're wondering why parents feel compelled to push children into some things, and steer them away from others, we can answer that by coming right back to the 16 desires. A parent with a powerful desire for *status, power*, and *physical activity*, might, for example, direct their kids into activities and behaviors that will match those desires. When the child in question happens to rate relatively low on those particular desires, you have a time bomb waiting to explode.

This reminds me of the story about the scorpion and the bullfrog. As a bullfrog sat next to the edge of a stream one day, a scorpion approached and said, "Hey man, I need to get to the other side." The frog snapped "No way, you're a scorpion, you'll sting me and I'll die!" "Hold on" spouted the scorpion, "I can't swim, that would be stupid...I'd die too!"

After considering the logic of the scorpion, the frog said "You're right, that wouldn't make sense, get on my back." With that, the scorpion hopped on and the frog began to swim towards the other side.

Just as the frog reached the midway point, the scorpion violently stung the frog! "What have you done?" gasped the frog, as he struggled to stay afloat. "I can't understand it. Why would you do that? Now we're both going to die!"

Just before they both slipped underwater, plunging to their certain deaths, the scorpion shouted "I'm a scorpion, and that's what scorpions do, we sting frogs!"

Does it seem that one of your children or perhaps your only child is your polar opposite? They may very well be, at least in terms of major desires. Our children will develop into the strong healthy adults they can become, when we support them in activities that fulfill their 16 desires, not ours.

Only when we understand ourselves in terms of the 16 basic desires, can we then begin to more fully understand, accept, and support others.

You can get a powerful overview of each of the sixteen basic desires in my audio program *Revealing Happiness* available at www.revealinghappiness.com. For a more thorough and complete analysis of this theory, however, I urge you to read the book, *Who Am I?* by Steven Reiss, Ph.D.

CHAPTER 22:

WHAT YOU CAN LEARN BY EAVESDROPPING AT MCDONALD'S

"We pray that the loss of life is very limited, but we fear that is not the case."

-Kathleen Blanco

A couple of weeks ago, my daughter and I were enjoying a nutritionally packed meal at McDonald's one afternoon, when I overheard one of the employees talking to someone about her recent compensation increase, "I'm more excited about the increase in my insurance than the pay raise!" she exclaimed. This, my friend, is at the heart of most of the decisions we make in life.

We are motivated by both pain and pleasure, but when it comes right down to it, we'll usually do far more to avoid pain than we will to gain pleasure.

You probably already know that human life isn't just pain and pleasure; we are in fact motivated by at least 16 basic desires, but for this particular section I'm just going to examine the role of pain and pleasure.

When someone needs to exercise each day to lose weight, but doesn't, the thought of exercising is exerting more pain than the thought of *not* exercising. It would seem that the only way out of this conundrum would be to eliminate the pain of not wanting to exercise, and let me tell you, I know a lot of fat people who fail miserably with that strategy. They convince themselves that when they get to the point that they don't wince when they think about exercise, they'll start. This is like standing on top of a big rock and trying to pick it up; from one perspective it seems like it should work, but it never will.

What can we do then? Pain can be associated to anything! The thought of quitting cold turkey when you've been a smoker for thirty years is most likely very painful, but I submit to you that no matter how much pain you're feeling, something else can always be more painful.

While working with a smoker in June of 2001, I was doing my initial "belief shattering" protocol with a lady who had been smoking two packs a day for nineteen years. I always start here; it's very common for someone to pay me a big chunk of money to quit smoking, and then show up with a firm belief that they can't do it. Therefore, I always liked to deal with that right off the bat. I asked her, "Will you agree to do anything I ask of you, as long as it won't cause you any harm?" She reluctantly agreed.

Even though I had no intentions of having her follow through this way, I said, "I want you to quit cold turkey today, with no help from me, for 48 hours, and then we'll do your first session. It will be tough, I know, but that's the deal." Her face revealed the obvious horror she was feeling inside. "I can't do that Vince! There's no (expletive) way; that's why I'm paying you!" "Yes, you are paying me" I said. "Presumably because you don't know what to do anymore, isn't that right? Everything you could think of has been done already, am I right? Why don't you think you can do it?" She was digging her heels in deeper and deeper with each question I asked.

Knowing that she had a nephew that was her heart and soul, I presented her with a scenario that suddenly changed what she would be able to do. "Are you telling me that if you walked into your house and a terrorist had Josh sitting tied up in a chair, with a gun pointed right at him, and he told you that if you smoked during the next 48 hours he would kill Josh, are you telling me that Josh had better be concerned?" Tears began to stream down her face, but they were tears of realization and empowerment. She knew instantly that she did, in fact, have the ability to choose not to smoke. She knew that she'd go through hell for a few days quitting cold turkey, but to save the life of her nephew, so what! "Hell yes! I could go 48 hours!" she said in a stern voice.

I simply attached pain to something else, something much more painful. By contrast the pain of the withdrawal became rather insignificant. After she had realized that she could gut her way through it if needed, she was ready to take a more humane approach, and work with me to eliminate the withdrawal symptoms and use her mind with laser like precision to lock the changes into place.

The pain of exercising is right now; the pain of seeing your family around your death bed is later...unless you are willing to experience it now. Those aren't things we feel very comfortable thinking about, so, we usually put them out of our mind as quick as they come. I've watched grown men be reduced to a puddle of tears when I take them through the experience of dying from lung cancer in the future -RIGHT NOW- in the present moment, as I help them make that as life like as possible. Once the agony of leaving young kids behind has been experienced fully, it's very difficult to simply push that thought aside any longer.

Our dear McDonald's lady was more excited about the insurance, something that she'd have to get sick to use, than she was about the pay increase that she could begin using right now. Do you think pain has a significant influence in our lives? What have you been associating pain to that has been limiting you? In what way could you attach *more* pain to not doing it, which by contrast would make it seem kind of silly?

Stop trying to eliminate pain, and begin to use it with as much precision as a surgeon uses a scalpel. Make pain your friend, and watch how many things in life suddenly become "possible" when you employ this strategy.

CHAPTER 23:

CHANGING BELIEFS WITH MOBY DICK

"If I have the belief that I can do it, I shall surely acquire the capacity to do it even if I may not have it at the beginning."

–Mahatma Ghandi

There are few things I enjoy as much as helping someone create new beliefs about their ability to change, and what they can expect to experience in the world in which they live. This is accomplished through any number of methods that have proven useful over the years, but there are some that stand out more than others, as I think back on some of my most "enjoyable" moments with clients.

It's hard to explain the feeling I experience as I watch someone go through an undeniable "ah ha" moment, and observe the "fogged out" look on their face as their brain works to re-organize, and create a new "structure" from which they will think in the future.

While complex linguistic or language patterns, various forms of hypnosis, and leading edge techniques of influence can work near miracles for conveying ideas to the "right" part of a client's brain, sometimes nothing beats letting someone physically engage in a process that will ultimately allow them to discover for themselves, what I might have otherwise told them.

Just around the corner from the room I usually see my clients in, is a large bookshelf that reaches from the floor to the ceiling, holding six different shelves of books. The only book with a red covering is the classic *Moby Dick*, with the large black letters of the title clearly written on its spine. All of the other books are blue, black, or some varied shade of one of these darker colors.

During a session, when the time seems right, I'll ask my client if they would go into the other room and get the book with the black cover, *Moby Dick*. Now, the act of just walking in and grabbing a book off of this shelf, and coming back into the room they had left, should take less than 30 seconds, and that's being really generous with the time allowance.

However, as I look at my watch, timing the process from the moment they get up, at least a full minute will go by, and then, I'll hear "Are you sure it's in here?" After assuring them, that, it is in fact there, and that all they need to do is look, I can sense their frustration building as they search in vain for the book I've asked for. I'll usually "save" them after 3-4 minutes, which to them, can seem like an eternity.

When I finally walk in the room, and pull the *red* book, with *Moby Dick* boldly written down the spine off the shelf, the responses are varied, but they are all some version of "Oh my god, I "saw" that book, I mean I looked right at it, but I didn't see those words on the spine!"

So what happened? I mean how is it that these intelligent people were able to scan their eyes across this book, but not "see" it? The answer is simple.

By telling them the cover of the book was black, I had set the frame of reference for how their brain would sort, as they scanned the many books held by this bookcase. Even though *Moby Dick* was the only book on that shelf that was red, or even close to red, and should have stood out like a bottle of low budget beer at a fine wine tasting event, it didn't.

Each time their eyes would move across the red book and their brain would detect the color red, the *delete* function kicked in and the words *Moby Dick* simply did not register. The brain had been instructed that the answer would only be found in a *black* book, and even though they had stopped and read the title of every dark colored book on that shelf, it never occurred to them to stop and read the title of the *red* book.

So let me ask you, what frames of reference have you instructed your brain to use for finding solutions? Have you unknowingly given your brain instructions that are the equivalent of a black covered book?

Let's look at another function of a frame of reference: *meaning*.

The frame of reference we hold will literally shape, alter and modify all incoming information. The recent firing of Don Imus at MSNBC is a tremendous example. Soon after Imus made the unfortunate remark, a poll at MSNBC showed that almost half of the people felt that the two week suspension was too harsh, and that this was what Imus was supposed to do as a "shock jock." The other half were all but calling for him to be beheaded, feeling that the only feasible solution was for him to be fired.

But we see this everywhere, don't we? Although it varies at any given time, overall, when you look at all of the polls taken regarding whether the U.S. should pullout of Iraq, or, whether we should stay and fight, we'll see that there's an average 50/50 split.

Should Imus have been fired? It depends on which half of the nation you ask. Should the U.S. stay and fight in Iraq? Again, it depends on which 50% you talk to.

Those who felt that Imus should be fired held a frame of reference that would "see" or identify with only that information which matched their "frame", and would delete, distort, deny, or simply not "see" or "hear" that which did not. What about those who felt he was just doing his job? Same thing; the "frame" held by these people will function in exactly the same way.

When you wish to persuade someone else, working (at least initially) within their frame of reference or their metaphor will produce staggering results. Trying to impose your frame upon theirs, however, will only result in a war of frames.

But let's talk about you. Let's momentarily forget about persuading others, and let's just think about how we can use this knowledge to positively work with our own lives. Do you know what your frames are? Let's start with one that is easy. Do you identify yourself as a Republican or a Democrat? Whatever your answer, the chosen party is your frame, and depending on the strength of your affiliation, you will refuse to even consider some to all of the ideas proposed by the other party.

This gets a little tricky. What are your frames regarding a marriage? Disciplining a child? Handling finances? Health, diet and exercise? Chances are, you know what you do regarding each of these areas, but my experience has been that very few people are aware of the frame of reference they have that drives these behaviors.

If you desire to change some aspect of your behavior, discovering the frames and beliefs that are behind the behavior can mean the difference between changing as smoothly as possible, and fighting against the current until finally, you collapse from exhaustion, and eventually drift back into the behavior you struggled to depart.

One of the easiest ways I know to determine what you believe about something, and thus what frame you hold, is to ask a series of questions that will remove the camouflage that has been concealing these powerful drivers of our behavior.

People generally reveal only one half of the structure of their belief. When someone says "Chevrolet Sucks, I'd never drive one!" we really have very little to work with. If, however, you simply use one magical little word, they will gladly hand over the other half of the belief; the half you need if you hope to help them reconstruct a more useful belief.

When someone says something like "Chevrolet sucks!" just look at them and say "because?" You'll then get the half that they use to support their first statement. "Because I was driving back from Tulsa late one night, in a Chevy Malibu I had at the time, and the damn thing broke down at 2:00 am in the middle of nowhere!"

Knowing this, there are countless ways you can now deconstruct the belief they have been using since the breakdown, and help them build another one, often times in simple conversation.

One of my favorites is presenting them with a counterexample. "Have you ever known *even one person* that drove a Chevy that *didn't* break down?" Here's another way to approach their faulty belief. "I'm wondering, do you think that in the history of Tulsa, there has ever been a Ford, Chrysler, Buick, or Toyota that broke down on the highway in the wee hours of the morning?"

You see, once you get the second half, it's relatively simple to cause someone's (or your own) belief to cave in on itself.

Can you see how listing all of your first half beliefs down one side of a paper, and then writing down the supporting half on the other side could allow you to see how weak some of your "supporting evidence" has been?

HERE'S AN EXAMPLE:

I will never be rich **because** *I don't have a college degree.*

I can't lose weight **because** *I don't like to exercise.*

When we allow ourselves to only focus on the first half, or the thoughts on the left side, we never call into play the "evidence" that has been backing up things from just below the surface. Once we do, though, once we call them out in the open where we can really scrutinize them, we'll often find ourselves delighted to discover how quickly we can punch these "reasons" full of holes.

CHAPTER 24:

TALK YOURSELF TO SLEEP

"Cats are rather delicate creatures and they are subject to a good many different ailments, but I have never heard of one who suffered from insomnia."

-Joseph Wood Krutch

From time to time someone will tell me they have been having trouble going to sleep at night. After asking them a few questions, if I determine that they are suffering from an overactive mind, listening to a seemingly endless flow of "inner chatter" as they try to get some shut eye, I'll take them through this remarkable little sleep inducing exercise.

Without fail, when I ask someone to go back in their mind to the last time they had trouble falling asleep, and then have them tune into what their inner voice sounded like as they were struggling to make their way into "la la land", they discover that it sounded like a teen age kid on too much caffeine, talking fast, loud, and in an almost anxious tone.

Now, here's the interesting part; not only can we instantly bring this part of our experience (our inner dialogue) that is most often just outside of our conscious awareness, into our conscious awareness, but we can then just as easily alter the structure of this inner voice, just by deciding to.

When I ask someone to imagine what their inner voice would sound like if they were so incredibly sleepy, that they just couldn't keep their eyes open, most are surprised not only by how easily they are able to "manipulate" this inner voice, but how quickly they begin to feel sleepy, even as they sit in my office in the middle of the day.

After instructing them on the importance of first altering their inner dialogue as they stretch out on their bed at night, I have them begin to imagine the sound of a crackling fireplace just a few feet from the foot of their bed. I suggest that they "listen" to the fire crackle and pop for at least 45-60 seconds, and then begin to allow an image of orange, yellow, and blue tinged flames, dancing in a fireplace to come together in their mind.

At this point, they can both "watch" and "listen" to the imaginary fireplace in their bedroom. They can now move to yet another sensory system, imagining the warmth of the fire warming the bottom of their out stretched feet.

Very few people ever make it all the way through this process before they fall deeply asleep. In fact, after they have been doing this procedure for a week or two, simply "hearing" their inner voice "talking" in a sleepy manner, this alone is often enough to put them down for the count, and many are unable to ever again get to the first step of the fireplace scene.

Of course, the fireplace is just one of an unlimited number of scenarios one could use to involve all of the senses; you could use literally anything that would invoke the thoughts and associations of things you have found relaxing in the past. But regardless of the scene you use, the key to the effectiveness of this technique can be found in the involvement of the auditory, visual, and kinesthetic or "feeling" part of the experience.

With just a little practice, you'll find that you can go to sleep just about anywhere, anytime you need to.

CHAPTER 25:

Don't Change Your Mind- Just Turn It Around

"I know you think I'm crazy. I go into a different room and I actually felt like it takes me to a better place, positive instead of negative."

-Martin Lawrence

If you wanted to have the tallest building in your town, there are two basic ways of approaching your goal; you could either measure the tallest building in town, and then set out to build one taller, or, you could tear down all of the other buildings, and whatever you build, regardless of the its height, yours will be the tallest one in town.

Clearly, tearing all of the other buildings down will require far more time and effort than simply building one that's taller than any of the others, but isn't that a good metaphor of what so many people do on a daily basis?

What would happen, if every time you started think about, or tell someone else why something would not work…you STOPPED… and then immediately asked the question "What are two good reasons why it *will* work?"

Better yet, you might want to use a method that Connirae Andreas calls reversing presuppositions. Let's say you were thinking about retiring and starting a flower shop, and each time you thought about it, you said something like, " But I really don't have any experience with running a flower shop, so that wouldn't work!"

Using Connirae's method, you would take the reason you had used to justify why it would not work, and turn it into a reason why it would.

Simply ask "How might the fact that I don't have any experience running a flower shop, actually be a reason why it would work?"

Because this question is so much different from the kind most people are used to asking, it will feel a bit strange, initially, but if you hang with it, you'll be amazed to find that your brain will actually begin supplying reasons, or answers to this question.

You might get an answer like "well, since you don't know anything about it, that means you don't have the limited thinking or bad habits that many florists or flower shop owners have acquired. Anything you need to know, you can learn. You won't have to try and undo a bunch of things that have been holding your flower shop back, like so many people would have to do if they wanted to take their shop to the next level. In this case, your ignorance is your best friend."

So many times in life, it comes down to the kind of questions that we ask. If we ask good questions we get good answers. Ask great questions, and get great answers. Far too many people have mastered the art of asking horrible questions, and as a result…you guessed it.

So tell me, why *will* your idea work? Anyone can tell you why it won't; break away from the norm, and discover why it *will*.

CHAPTER 26:

HYPNOTIZED BY AN 11 YEAR OLD UNDER A MAPLE TREE

"Jose has been key to our depth at catcher. He has developed a good rapport with our pitching staff."

-Bill Stoneman

How many times have you met someone for only a few moments, but something about the interaction left you feeling like you had known them for years? I'll never forget that July day in the summer of 1977; I was putting the "sissy bar" back on my bike, so that I could get back to the ramp I had built in a attempt to pull off a stunt I felt would rival that of one of my heroes, Evel Knievel, when a kid that had been in my class at school walked up into the yard.

Although I knew Tommy, I'd really never had much of a conversation with him before. He was on his way to McCarty's Market, a little grocery store about a block down the street from where I lived on 428 W. 13th St. in Trenton, Missouri, and had noticed me playing out in the front yard.

Thirty years later, I couldn't tell you one single word Tommy spoke that day, but if I live to be 100 years old, I'll forever remember how I felt. I had no idea what had happened, I literally felt as if I was standing across from a mirror image of myself, and that somehow Tommy seemed to only be speaking when he knew the words he would say, were the words I would choose if I was the one talking. Never before, in any of the previous 11 years of my life could I remember having been so relaxed and at ease. Every sign of tension had drained from my body, and all I wanted to do was listen to him talk. When he finally had to dash off to get the hand sliced lunch meat his mother had sent him to get for lunch,

I remember just standing under the cool shade of that beautiful old Maple tree, enjoying the feelings of comfort that were whirling through my mind and body.

Twenty two years later, I would discover exactly what had happened on that long ago summer afternoon. While I'm quite sure Tommy had no idea of what he was doing on a conscious level, and in fact, was just being himself, I had discovered that it was possible to duplicate the effect that Tommy had created for me that day, in virtually anyone, when you knew how.

What I had experienced that day was the synchronization between Tommy and me, of several aspects of my behavior that were just outside of my conscious awareness. Things like my breathing, the rate and speed of my voice (both externally and internally), my posture, and countless other behavioral factors, were being mirrored back to me by Tommy as he visited with me that afternoon.

On some other than conscious level, my brain was saying, "Hey, this feels very familiar–this person is just like me." Familiarity is a very powerful driving force in human beings. We have a propensity to like, agree with, and move towards things that, are, or seem familiar, and we usually experience an increase in tension and resistance, and rapidly move away from things that are unfamiliar.

It is important, then, to understand that the level of rapport we have with others, or how familiar and "acceptable" we seem to them when interacting, will very often be the difference that makes the difference. When others like and/or feel comfortable with us, they will most likely be willing to take another step forward with the interaction, whatever that step may be. In the event that we have not been able to establish rapport, and the other person is feeling uncomfortable or uneasy with us, we'll find trying to take the conversation to another level challenging at best. It has been my experience that until we have received feedback indicating that others are feeling comfortable with us, our time should be utilized for the sole purpose of creating this much needed level of comfort and trust.

Fortunately, the process of establishing trust with others need not take long at all. By intentionally and systematically learning to employ the mannerisms that my friend Tommy was naturally engaging in that afternoon, we can not only create a feeling of openness in others, but it can make the interaction more comfortable and enjoyable for us as well.

Now, that's fine and dandy, and, one can learn to master the matching and mirroring of another person's breathing, eye blinks, gestures, facial expressions, muscle tension, voice qualities, and countless other behaviors...but...it takes systematic practice and dedication to accomplish the level of mastery that operates for the most part, on an unconscious level.

About a year ago, I discovered something that slices through the muck of learning to establish rapport, and will allow someone to instantly create the same level of rapport with another person, that someone who has trained for years to achieve using other methods.

I am all about simplicity, call it laziness if you want, I'm very comfortable with that "label" if it means getting more done with less effort. Growing up in a farming community, I know all too well what it means to earn your spending money in high school "bucking" hay bales in 100 degree temperatures in the mid day sun. Even from an early age, I never understood the seeming "bravado" of the older men professing proudly how hard they work to earn their money. It didn't make sense then, and it sure doesn't make sense today. Mastery is about finding the most efficient way to achieve something, and even then, continuing to look for an even better way.

So then, what is it that creates such an intense level of rapport? The "technique" is simple, so I'm going to keep the explanation simple. If you are accessing the appropriate states, you will also be manifesting the needed physiological counterparts of that state. NLP promotes matching a person's mannerisms and physical movements, even if those movements aren't born from a state that will be conducive to them feeling wonderful. While this certainly can work, it eats up a lot of unnecessary time and energy.

If the state you are accessing is strong enough, it will penetrate the roughest of "defense" perimeters put up by others. When I work with a client, I may start "where" they are as far as belief systems are concerned, but I have no desire to access the less than resourceful states they walked in with. I access the state I want them to gravitate towards, the minute they step out of the car. "Enough already-what is it!" you might be thinking.

THE STATE OF GRATITUDE AND APPRECIATION

When you have adequately accessed these states, there won't be any reason to think about your facial expressions, gestures, breathing, etc. You will be displaying so many powerful signals with your non-verbal communication that it's just not even conceivable that the other person won't be impacted in a positive way.

This is real simple; there are just a few steps for accessing these states, and once you're "there" the effect will last for at least an hour, and this will become longer and longer with use.

First, allow your lower jaw to drop down ½ -1 inch, so that your jaw is loose and relaxed. Next, look at something in front of you, and while keeping your eyes and head pointed in that direction, shift your attention or awareness into your peripheral vision. Notice, and become aware of what's just off to the sides, just below, and just above.

Loosening the jaw assists you in disengaging from your internal chatter and helps your mind go quiet. Shifting to your peripheral vision will stimulate your parasympathetic nervous system. As odd as it may sound, when the parasympathetic nervous system is stimulated, it actually causes you to relax.

Now you're ready to close your eyes, and take your awareness to the area that surrounds your heart. Just take it there and focus on this space in your chest for 15-20 seconds. By now, you will have noticed a tremendous shift and softening in your state of mind and body. While continuing to hold your attention here, think about someone that you love and appreciate unconditionally. Just let the feelings of love and gratitude you have about this person flood your entire being. (If you don't get a powerful shift here, use the thought of someone else until you do)

You can hold this feeling as long as you want or have time for, and when you are ready to move to the next step, simply think about the person you will be working or communicating with, while holding on, fully and completely to the previous feeling of love and appreciation. When this is done just moments before meeting with this person, the "aura" that will be vibrating from you will be an undeniable force, and they'll have no choice but to feel the message you're sending.

Do I do this with everyone I meet? No, I don't. I usually reserve this for family and clients. Once you have used this method with a number of people, you'll see what I mean. It's powerful enough that I just don't want to connect with everyone I meet on that level, and chances are, after you experience its power, you won't either. Oh, but what a tool to have, when you do want or need to connect that deeply!

Chapter 27:

You'd Never Put up with This from Someone Else

"Self-Sabotage is when we say we want something and then go about making sure it doesn't happen."

-Alyce P. Cornyn-Selby

There are very few adults that don't know the misery that comes from being at war with themselves. For countless reasons, most men and women make it to adulthood with a wide range of disparaging comments they say to themselves each day. Fortunately, it's not necessary to be able to pinpoint the place, time and people in our past that contributed to our unconscious adoption of the self defeating statements and inner dialogue.

"I just don't deserve to be here" or "I'm not as pretty, handsome, skilled, or liked as the other people in this group." Internal statements like this are only strengthened when we argue with them; it's a vicious circle that spins us round and round on a ride of bitterness and discontent.

Traditional wisdom (by now you know I'm anything but traditional) tells us that the only way to "win" an argument, is to simply refuse to enter into one in the first place. While this may very well work for the conversations in our external world, this strategy strips us of a very powerful skill when dealing with "conversations" in our internal world.

Dr. Steven Reiss, a psychology professor at the *University of Ohio*, and the author of *Who am I? The 16 Basic Desires that Motivate Our Actions and Define Our Personalities* wrote about the power of vengeance when it comes to motivation. Initially, many people wrinkle their noses at the thought of vengeance having a useful purpose, but in fact, Reiss found that vengeance spills over into areas that are commonly accepted by many as "noble." Competition is one such example.

Time and time again, I have observed men and women who weren't necessarily role models for great self-esteem, vehemently reject a derogatory comment from someone else, and verbally argue to the ends of the earth that the other person is wrong. Perhaps someone calls them a "worthless, lazy bum-a no- good loser!" and what happens next is predictable; "Who are you calling worthless? You are too stupid to know anything, let alone making a judgment about me, *you* are the one that's stupid!"

Are you beginning to see the difference in how we treat the comments coming from others, and those that we generate ourselves? More importantly, have you caught a glimpse of the power this knowledge holds for self transformation?

Before I reveal this wonderful little gem, let me say this; I don't view any technique, however powerful and effective it may be, as a stand-alone method for change. In fact, my audio program, *Revealing Happiness* is a collection of multiple principles and methods of self-transformation, as I think any good program offers a vast array of possibilities for the man or woman wanting a change in their life. We are far too unique as individuals to think that everyone will benefit from exactly the same technique.

Experience has shown that a much better strategy is to provide many different techniques, methods and principles that have all proven their effectiveness, and present them in a format that will allow the end-user to use some, or all of it, based upon what they need at that time in their lives. Therefore, know that what you will learn here is just one of many amazingly effective techniques for modifying or amplifying your experience of life.

In one particular session, a client of mine kept repeating, "I always find myself thinking that I don't deserve to succeed." I said, "Let me ask you something. Was there anyone in high school that you just couldn't stand?" She quickly nodded and acknowledged that there was indeed someone that she had detested. I had her close her eyes and imagine that this high school "foe" was standing in front of her, waving her finger in her face and saying, "You don't deserve to succeed!"

As she did this, I could see her entire physiology shift into a more confident and aggressive posture, and out of the weak and submissive look she had displayed seconds before. "Give me a report on what you're thinking and feeling as you imagine this scenario." I said. My client quickly snapped, "I'm thinking, you little rip! Who the hell do you think you are to tell me what I deserve? I deserve anything I want, and I can create anything I want!!"

Amazing isn't it; if all it takes to garner our deepest resources and kick our butts into gear, is to have someone else try and tell us we can't, or that we don't deserve to, then why in the world don't we use the unlimited power of our imagination to put this into action now?

HERE ARE STEP BY STEP INSTRUCTIONS FOR DOING THAT VERY THING:

1. Identify something that you routinely say to yourself that tends to deflate you a bit and that more often than not, you find yourself agreeing with.
2. From any time frame in your life, think of someone that you have thought of as annoying, and whose ideas you would reject as nonsense.
3. Imagine this person telling you the same thing you had earlier identified as the non-resourceful statement you had been making to yourself.

I can tell you this, I have watched people take self- defeating comments they had fought with for years, and vaporize them in a matter of days, just by employing this supercharged method, and then immediately using it to zap any new inner comments that may surface later.

CHAPTER 28:

THINKING FROM A HIGHER LEVEL

"You can never solve a problem on the level on which it was created."

-Albert Einstein

Those who know me well know that I vigorously promote the idea that there are no "good" feelings or emotions, or "bad" feelings or emotions. There are only "useful" or "non-useful" feelings and emotions, and until you can answer the question "useful or non-useful for who, where, and when?" you can't very well know which category the emotion or feeling at hand fits into.

People are quick to judge anger as a "bad" emotion. This changes in an instant though, if you ask them if it is still a "bad" emotion, if their 12 year old child avoids being raped, because she disapproved of the comments a would be rapist was using, and after becoming angry, notified a nearby adult of the offensive and lewd comments of the man or woman in question. They'll often say, "Well, in that case, it would be different!" Yes, it would be different in that case, just as it is in any case, because the usefulness of everything depends on the context.

We often think of a "paranoid" as being what someone is, more often than not however, it would be more accurate to use this label to describe one's patterned style of thinking. Learning to understand the structure of such thought patterns can be very beneficial, not only for those who tend to engage in this manner of processing information, but for those who have frequent contact with those who are producing thoughts and feelings that result from this disrupting flow of data.

Before we dive in, though, it's important to understand what is referred to as "logical levels" or thinking from higher levels. Albert

Einstein once said that "a problem cannot be solved on the same level that it exists" and this is exactly what he was referring to. I might add that a less than useful utilization of logical levels can also take a problem that doesn't exist, and create "thought demons" that throw your nervous system into a tizzy.

Logical levels might best be described as "aboutness." Using the "ladder" metaphor, when you have a thought *about* a previous thought, you have just gone up to the next "rung", or to a "higher" level of thinking. Although various people will agree or disagree with the following, my definition of a logical level is the first level of thinking that involves "aboutness", and that no longer relies solely on raw sensory input.

What is sensory input? If you see a handgun in the middle of your living room floor upon entering you home, sensory input is nothing more than the visual information you register when you first see the gun. Further sensory data might consist of the coolness of the metal or the weight of the gun as you lift it, or, if you pull back the hammer, the sensory input may also be comprised of a sound. This is referred to by psychologist Michael Hall, as primary awareness.

Enter the first logical level; you now think to yourself, "What is this gun doing in my house?" This thought *about* what your senses have detected, generates both a search for meaning, as evidenced by either the question, " What is this gun doing here?" or the simple recognition, " There's a gun in my house." You have now had thoughts *about* the gun.

Jumping to the second logical level, you now have the opportunity to categorize the gun. This is where we find a huge discrepancy from one person to the next, in the meanings they will assign to the gun. From this logical level, someone with a teenage son might think, "That's scary; my son is planning to kill himself!" Yet another person may simply think "That kids at it again, he's always buying something and leaving it laying around-he's so irresponsible" While yet another might think, "Someone has broken into the house, and there's been a fight here in the living room-they've kidnapped my son!" As you may have already surmised, the available meanings we could assign to what our senses have detected are only limited by our imagination, which is to say, it's limitless.

Now, even when a less than useful meaning has been assigned on logical level two, *about* what we have seen, heard, smelled, tasted, or felt when we walked into the room, the intensity of our response/reaction in terms of our behavior and feelings, will largely hinge upon what occurs on the third logical level.

The level of certainty a person has *about* the thoughts they had on the second logical level are all important. Please note that the thoughts on this level are even further away from the level of primary information than the thoughts on level two. Also, notice that the thoughts on level two may very well make up what the person is calling the problem. The man or woman that thinks, "Cool, John has used his money wisely, and bought something that will hold value, instead of spending it on drugs" will not be experiencing a "problem" about what they have detected. The same cannot be said of the person who thinks, "My son is thinking of killing himself." The "problem" this person will experience, will have been initially generated by their thoughts *about* the gun, or what it *means* to them.

If, after having assigned a meaning on level two, a person has feelings of certainty about those thoughts, they will have strengthened and solidified the level two thoughts and feelings, neurologically speaking.

The number of times we can reflect on something, or, the number of logical levels we can ascend regarding some sensory based event, is unlimited. Therefore, it is crucial that we understand this: each new or "higher" logical level thought, governs, modifies and alters all that are below it. This understanding offers tremendous insight, then, to the logical level we might work from when wanting to create a change in ourselves or others.

When I am certain that the gun *means* my son is planning to commit suicide, I allow no other thoughts in at that point, and if someone attempts to persuade me otherwise, I will vehemently defend my position.

If, however, my sons possible suicide plot enters my mind, but my thoughts and feelings on the third logical level are a bit shaky, or uncertain, my mind will still entertain other possible explanations, and I'll be less likely to begin acting on any certain thought or explanation until I have investigated the matter more fully. This by the way is truly a mark of a healthy style of thinking.

How can we break out of this loop, or assist another to escape the trap of certainty, when the power of our affirmation is producing "crazy" like or unfounded behavior? For this we can often rely on the "magic" of paradox. Paradox "jams" things up a bit, and quite paradoxically, then, frees our thinking and behaving.

There is an ancient story that peeved theologians and philosophers, due to the fact that it was seemingly impossible to work with. According to the story, the devil once asked God to create a rock so large that even God himself couldn't lift it. If God could not lift the rock, he would no longer be omnipotent; if he could lift it, that would only mean he was unable to make one big enough that he could not lift it. How can we use the structure of paradox then?

Let's look at this example used by a particular therapist:

Therapist: Are you sure of that?

Client: Yes.

Therapist: Are you sure you're sure?

Client: Yes.

Therapist: Are you sure enough to be UNSURE?

Notice that after he has asked this question, no matter what answer they give him, they have just "loosened" the "grip" of the thoughts and beliefs that had been limiting their thinking so tightly. If they say, "Yes, I'm sure enough to be unsure" they have accepted that they are somewhat unsure. If they say, "No, I'm not sure enough to be unsure" They have expressed doubt, and have once again, accepted that they are somewhat unsure.

So let me ask you, what are you sure enough of to be unsure about? Or, perhaps there's something that you're not sure enough about to be unsure of. Think deeply on this, I'm sure you'll find it to be as liberating as I have, or the countless clients I have used this with to loosen their thoughts.

Strategically thinking *about* your thinking can be a bit challenging initially. However, once you have been able to see just how effort-lessly you have already been *unconsciously* using this structure, you'll soon be re-orchestrating your thinking, taking conscious control, and I think you'll find yourself thinking that Einstein was right.

CHAPTER 29:

FACING CHANGES BY CHANGING FACES

"A smile confuses an approaching frown."

-Unknown

You've no doubt heard someone talking about "laughing hyenas" or, if you grew up in a rural area in the Midwest like I did, you've also heard or used the phrase "grinning like a possum." Now, I have to admit, I have absolutely no idea what the emotional state of a hyena or possum might be when they have a "grin" or "smile" on their face. However, if I were to use what research has shown us over and over again, coupled with my own subjective experience, and apply that to the hyena and opossum, then clearly, I would tell you that the hyena and opossum would probably be happier than most other animals.

I urge you to make it a point to "check in" on the status of your face every fifteen minutes for a day, just to see how often you're smiling, or not. You might be surprised to discover how often you have the polar opposite; many people spend the largest part of their day, working with some form of "scowl", a "scrunched" tense face, or something along those lines that corresponds with a less that "positive" or happy state of mind and body.

I could cite many studies that show a powerful correlation between our facial expressions and our level of happiness, or what moods or emotions we are experiencing. But why would I want to do that? You can experience it for yourself…right now!

Simply raise the corners of your mouth, allowing a gentle and easy smile to spread across your face, and while this is happening, allow this to "soften" your eyes. Now, simply hold this for thirty seconds.

If you actually took the time to do this exercise, you now know firsthand, just how powerful this is. The shift that you feel is real; by changing the expression on our face, we are simultaneously altering the biochemistry of our body.

I remember a quote I read years ago that said, "They do not sing because they are happy, they are happy because they sing." The same can be said of a smile; don't wait to "be happy" before you smile, go ahead and start smiling now, and find out how close behind "happiness" might be.

Something you might find very beneficial is to put a soft and subtle smile on your face, and then, while holding that expression, go ahead and think of some challenge that had been worrying you. I think you'll find that the "challenge" takes on a different feeling- one that is more conducive to happiness and productivity.

CHAPTER 30:

HAVE YOU GONE OVER YOUR THRESHOLD?

"True love is like a pair of socks; you gotta have two and they've gotta match."

-Unknown

Chances are good that at some point in your life you have experienced a sudden realization that you were living your life around someone else's plans; you suddenly develop an awareness that more decisions in your life than you care to remember, have been determined by someone other than yourself.

Now, this may be in the context of your career, interactions with extended family or neighbors, or a marriage. One thing is certain; when there is harmony in the relationship, we are comfortable having others "weigh in" on the decision, making a cooperative determination. And isn't it true, that when the relationship is really harmonious, that we don't even mind having an occasional decision made "for" us, by the person in question?

How do we know when the relationship is no longer harmonious? John Gottman, Ph. D., the world's foremost expert on the "success" or "failure" of marriages feels that this harmony exists when we feel respected. Using sophisticated video cameras, Gottman has been able to predict with 91% accuracy which couples will be divorced within 4-6 years, by watching them interact on camera, and then using the findings of world renowned facial expression scientist, Paul Ekman, to interpret the "communication" between them. Where there is consistent "contempt" shown by one or both of the partners toward the other, the "show" is pretty much over. Again, Gottman has consistently predicted with 91% accuracy, who will "make it", and who won't.

Much of it has to do with what I call going over *threshold*. Let's say that from time to time, your computer just shuts down, you have no idea why, it just does. Now, if this only happens once every two weeks, even though it's a royal pain in the butt, you'll probably go a long time before you finally "feel" like you *need* to buy a new one. Let this same thing start happening once a day, though, and it won't be long before you toss it through the window and head off on your new computer search.

Perhaps threshold would be better described like this; imagine a long glass tube, about 8 inches in diameter, and six feet long, resting vertically against a wall in your home. Much like a giant thermometer, it has a semi-thick red liquid that rises when you are upset or angry.

Let's pretend that we are starting at a baseline, where all of the red liquid is pooled at the bottom of the tube. Enter the first experience where your partner makes some "cutting" remark; the red liquid now comes up about two feet in the tube. Naturally, given enough time before the next "hurtful" remark by this other person, your anger will have had time to dissipate, and the red liquid will have returned to its starting position.

Wait a minute though, what about the situation where your "red liquid" has come up two feet, and has only gone about half way back down before the next sarcastic or contemptuous remark comes your way? Now the red liquid, even if it only travels the normal two feet, is now pushing to the three foot mark.

Then, if once again, before the "liquid" has had a chance to go back down, BAM-you are angered or hurt again. What happens?

This pattern will eventually "ratchet" the red liquid all the way to the top, and then, much like the proverbial cartoon thermometer in an overheated room...BOOM!

When this happens with a human being, I call it going over threshold. Once we have gone past our threshold, by having experienced too many of the same emotions in a compressed period of time, we experience an emotional "pop." Just as a bubble that has "popped" can no longer return to its previous form, neither can most of us ever return to the same feelings we had before the "pop."

We often hear this expressed with such phrases as "I just don't feel anything for them anymore" or "It's just not there, it's gone, it's like I'm numb."

Comments like this are a verbal description of the emotional landscape of a person's inner world. Can people "hold" a relationship together once they hit this point? I think you would agree, that people can hold it together even in the bleakest of conditions when they let the fear of the unknown control their destiny.

Women who have been beaten once a month for ten years will often stay around, simply because they know what to expect. My god, if they left and went elsewhere, it might be different, and they wouldn't have the same degree of predictability in their lives for some time, and that folks, is often enough, the fear of the unknown.

Will most people be able to experience the passion and peak emotional experiences they desire in life, "holding" a situation like this together? I'll leave that one for you to answer.

CHAPTER 31:

TRUTH OR CONSEQUENCES

"A lie would have no sense unless the truth were felt as dangerous."

-Alfred Adler

Early in the spring of 2008, I had one of the most adrenaline provoking experiences I'd had in over a decade. I had the opportunity to ride with the Missouri State Highway Patrol, doing drug interdiction along Interstate 35 (I-35), in Northwest Missouri. Starting the shift at 3:00 a.m., the Patrolman I was riding with was accompanied on the road by another Patrolman, driving the K-9 Unit car, with a German Sheppard that had a look in his eyes that said, "Go ahead, and make my day!"

When you make a traffic stop after having "jumped" across the median, and then race at nearly 130 mph to catch up with the targeted vehicle, your blood is more than adequately pumping through your system. Now, add the fact that it's still black as coal outside, and the vehicle you've pulled over has tinted windows, leaving you only to detect an unknown number of people moving about inside, and you have a Missouri State Highway Patrolman with cause for being on an extremely high-alert status.

The traffic violations that triggered a stop were varied, but in general, it was for excessive speed, expired plates, or driving (rather than passing) in the passing lane on the Interstate. This was a new insight for me, as I had a habit of driving in that lane just to get a better view of what was ahead...oops. Once the driver of the car was seated in the front seat of the patrol car (with me having moved to the back seat), the fun would begin.

The patrolman I was riding with had developed a very successful strategy of questioning over the years. It allows him to intuitively know whether or not he should move forward, asking for permission to search their vehicle. In the state of Missouri, you do not have to give them permission, but they do reserve the right to have the K-9 officer walk the dog around your vehicle nonetheless, and if he "hits" while sniffing, that's probable cause, and the search is on.

He would begin with simple questions; questions like, "Where do you live?" "Where do you work?" "Where are you going?" It wasn't so much the answer to the initial question that offered any useful feedback. Whenever they would answer, he would then ask a question about that answer, and then the next, and so on. If the initial answer they gave was nothing more than B.S. designed to throw him off of their "real" reason for traveling on this day, it would soon become obvious, as each subsequent answer took more and more processing time, since they were having to make up new answers, trying to make sure they all related logically to the original answer....and that's hard to do.

A typical conversation went something like this:

Patrolman: "Where you going today?"
Driver: "To visit a friend."
Patrolman: "Where does your friend live?"
Driver: "In Lansing, Michigan."
Patrolman: "Really, I'm somewhat familiar with that area, what street does he live on?"
Driver: (there is a noticeable delay in answering) "On the south side, I can't really remember the exact street address; I just kind of know the landmarks."
Patrolman: (this question is critical) "How long has your friend lived there?"
Driver: "About 9 months, now... I'm not really sure, maybe a year."
Patrolman: "So what are you guys going to do?"
Driver: "I think we're going to go camping."
Patrolman: "When was the last time you were up there?"
Driver: "It was a couple of years ago."
Patrolman: "Oh, so you have been there before then? I mean that's how you know how to get there, with the landmarks and all?"

Driver: "That's right."

Patrolman: "Question; you said he's only lived there 9 months to a year, and yet you drove there about two years ago?"

Driver: (with a look of obvious confusion and panic setting in) "Why are you asking so many questions?"

Patrolman: "Would it be okay with you if we search your vehicle?"

Driver: "I'd rather you not, I'd prefer you just give me my ticket so I can get on my way?"

It was at this point that the K-9 officer arrived, and the show began.

There are tons of books on deception or lie detection; the books are filled with elaborate techniques for trying to decipher whether someone is telling the truth, or not. Isn't it true, that there have been times in your life that knowing whether someone was lying would have been helpful? Wouldn't you want to "know" if your kids had just come home from the mall, or if instead, were hanging out with a known drug dealer?

Unfortunately, there is no method I know of that will allow us to read the minds of our children so we can better protect them. We can however, use our awareness to notice how smoothly others are responding to our questions about the answers they give us, to get a really strong "gut" feeling about the accuracy of the information being delivered.

The wonderful part about this is that you can use it without seeming like you are an interrogator. Used with the right voice tone and body language, you can even come across as someone who is genuinely interested and curious. Most people never get to feel that they have truly been listened to. When they finally sense that someone *is*, in fact, interested in what they have to say, they'll open up and chatter like a chipmunk. I fully advocate first accessing a state of genuine curiosity, as this it will help generate the needed non-verbal signals.

As with everything else I write about, I trust that you'll use this information for good and useful outcomes for both yourself and others. I invite you to discover the power of quickly asking questions about the previous answer, and doing so until you are satisfied that they are "shooting" straight with you.

CHAPTER 32:

DID HE JUST ASK ME A QUESTION?

"One who asks a question is a fool for five minutes; one who does not ask a question remains a fool forever."
  -Chinese Proverb

What in the world does asking questions have to do with captivating your audience? Everything! Imagine the feeling of being able to hold the attention of everyone you're speaking or presenting to, whether it is one or one thousand. The fact is, unless you can keep all eyes and ears riveted on you while you're presenting, your message will be watered down at best.

One of the most powerful uses of language for securing attention without coming across as "pushy" is the use of "hidden questions." Direct questions can sometimes seem a bit blunt; we have a tendency to resist someone we feel is trying to probe and inquire too much. Asking questions in a certain way, however, can be used to bypass the resistance that is often inherent when asking direct questions.

If for example, you ask, "How many people in here today have run a red light recently?" you may trigger some nervousness or resentment among the audience members. By changing the way you "ask" that question, they won't even know a question has been asked. If you say, "Now, I don't know how many of you have run a red light recently…" A very different experience will unfold. Let's examine what happens when it's "asked" in this manner.

The listeners mind will access the exact same thing. Think of it like this; if you ask the question directly, they'll think about whether they have run a light or not. Using the hidden question causes them to think the very same thing, with one *huge* difference; they feel as though *they decided* to think about it when you use the power of hidden questions.

Powerful communicators have always known how effective questions can be for capturing the attention of others. They also know that sometimes, questions, when asked directly, can backfire. Begin today, and insert hidden questions into your conversations and presentations, and watch how much warmer those who are listening become.

Chapter 33:

Why the Words "Vince Harris" Are the Most Powerful Words in the World

"You can make more friends in two months by becoming interested in other people than you can in two years by trying to get other people interested in you."

-Dale Carnegie

Why are the words Vince Harris the most persuasive words in the world? For the same reason the words of your name are the most persuasive words in the world to you; all other words fall short of the power of your name for captivating you, and riveting your attention on the person who spoke those words.

While I had always been aware of the effect of calling someone by their first name, it wasn't until about 4 years ago, that Lanny Master's introduced me to an extreme version of this communication tool.

Lanny had a peculiar, but powerful way of using a person's name while telling a story. One day he was going on about a car he used to have, telling me all about the engine, tires etc. Now, I normally find talking about cars about as interesting as watching paint dry, but on this particular afternoon, I was truly interested in what he was saying, and actually learned a great deal.

Lanny elaborated on the massive engine under the hood of his self-created hot rod, "I mashed down on the gas, those tires started spinning and Vince Harris, I'm telling you, the power of that car was mind blowing..."

About once every 1-2 minutes, Lanny would insert my name, "And Vince Harris..." Just hearing my full name every few moments was enough to interest me in something that I normally found painfully boring. Because someone that speaks both our first *and* last name, is something we usually never hear, it just made it stand out all that much more.

Do you want to command and then keep the attention of others? Begin using their full name as you speak. For me, hearing "Vince Harris" was music to my ears, and I assure you that others will find the melodic value in their name as well.

Chapter 34:

Are They Really Mad or Are You Really Wrong?

"Somebody must take a chance. The monkeys who became men, and the monkeys who didn't are still jumping around in trees making faces at the monkeys who did."

-Lincoln Steffens

Who among us has not experienced the feelings of rage, insecurity, fear, or some other "negative" emotion that was triggered by a certain "look" from someone else? If a waitress gives you a look that just doesn't "settle" well, it probably won't be a big deal; it may not be comfortable, but it's not like you have to see her every day.

However, if this look is chronic, showing up on a consistent basis, from someone you see daily, this same "look" might present a challenge. Encounter this "look" from a spouse or significant other on a regular basis, and you have the makings of what we refer to as a "tussle" here in the Midwest.

Unfortunately, all too often our misinterpretation of the facial expressions of others leads to unnecessary turmoil. Odd as it may seem, many of those who have been married for years, have never correctly identified the non-verbal messages offered by their spouse.

It's important to note, that the primary reason for these chronic misinterpretations, is that this all takes place on an unconscious level, just below the threshold that would allow us to notice and make clearer distinctions.

Therapists and counselors who have been divorced are often ridiculed for offering marriage advice to others. But let me share something with you; if you truly want to learn how to enhance your marriage, find someone who has been divorced, or who has had a very rocky marriage, but then turned things around and now enjoys a truly fulfilling relationship.

Forget about finding a couple that has always had a stable relationship, and asking them how they do it. Why? It's really rather simple. Success is a very poor teacher.

When things are going well, we rarely stop to question why things are running so smoothly. Instead, we just enjoy the fruits of our unconscious labor and almost always struggle when pressed to reveal the real strategies behind our success.

Those who have turned things around, on the other hand, have been "prodded" by the pain of their previous condition. They discover and bring into their conscious awareness, the patterns of behavior that were responsible for their strife. Then, they maintain that heightened state of awareness as they methodically integrate new and improved behaviors and habits, thus affording them the opportunity to tell others precisely what they do that creates the happiness they experience.

Those who are the happiest in their marriage and/or relationships have mastered the skill of "reading" the face of those they are close to. While this topic alone could take an entire book, you don't have to know everything to be able to benefit tremendously.

John Gottman, the world's foremost researcher on successful marriages offers the following four keys to think about. Utilizing these keys can enhance your people reading skills and your ability to empower your relationships to unbelievable levels of unity and bliss:

1. **Identify what the persons face looks like when they are in a neutral state:** You have to have a baseline to work from. It's a whole lot easier to distinguish one expression from another, and more importantly, what it "means", when you know what a "clean slate" face for this person looks like.

2. **Realize that people generally experience more than one emotion:** What you observe on the face of another is often a confusing mixture of several different emotions at one. If they are trying to conceal their feelings, it gets even trickier. Therefore, thinking someone is mad, sad, happy, etc. may only be partially true.

3. **Don't mistake habitual facial features as temporary emotions signals:** Some people are "blessed" with mouths that have down turned corners, and they appear to be unhappy just about all of the time. Clearly identify the natural expressions that might have been easily misinterpreted as meaning something that didn't do much to enhance the feelings between the two of you.

4. **Slow down, and really LOOK:** Since most emotions are fleeting, and facial expressions speed past us in somewhat of a blur at times, it's important that we develop our observational skills over time, with practice, just like we do with any other worthwhile endeavor. Look, really look, at the face of the other person or loved one when you are communicating with them. When you're uncertain what a look "means" ASK THEM what it means, or what they were feeling just then. As obvious as that seems, it's amazing how many people never do it. They're so certain that they already know what it means, that they don't ever validate it with a simple question.

You've probably already thought of several instances where you wound up in a full blown argument with someone you love, simply because on an unconscious level, the look on their face triggered something deep inside you. Perhaps the memory of an abusive parent, or a bully at school, was triggered by a similar look on their face as they were taunting you. With associations like this taking place, especially outside of your conscious awareness, it's a given that you'll be needlessly enduring upsets and arguments, over and over again.

While there are many other, far more powerful strategies that the happiest couples utilize, the best place to start is with the very simple, but amazingly effective fundamentals. As the fundamentals go, ceasing to allow a loved one's facial expressions to thrust you into overdrive is as basic as it gets.

Enjoy making these discoveries, expanding your awareness of the impact that a simple look from another can have on you, and watch what happens to your relationships!

CHAPTER 35:

DEALING WITH REALITY ONCE AND FOR ALL

"Reality is the only word in the English language that should always be used in quotes."

-Unknown

A recent discussion with someone who had years ago, gone to several marriage counseling sessions with her husband, highlighted one very important, but sadly, not so well known fact. Knowing this fact can make your journey through life very enjoyable and productive. However, failing to understand, remember and then implement this fact will all but guarantee a life of hell on earth. But before I reveal this fact, let me set the stage.

This woman talked of the day the counselor asked her husband how he "knew" that what he had stated as one of his complaints earlier was true. Hesitantly, he acknowledged that he didn't "know" for sure, and admitted he had no evidence to support his assertion. However, he continued to say that it was what he thought to be the cause of the problem.

Once we are convinced of something, our imagination can run away with us. Whether you are imagining the mail man having a steamy affair with your wife, or the sexy little vixen at the cosmetic counter running her fingers through your husband's hair, you are processing it with the very same part of the brain that would be at work if you actually witnessed the "real" thing.

Don't believe it? Go to your spouse and stand directly in front of them, close enough that you can see the pupils of their eyes. Then, ask them to imagine they are standing on top of a roof and suddenly slip and fall. Watch their eyes. Their pupils will constrict and become much smaller momentarily- just like they would if they were really on the roof.

Our nervous system responds just as powerfully to the pictures and movies that we run through our head each day (consciously and unconsciously) as it does to the actual experience we have, or the things we really see in the external world around us.

Jealousy is a very misunderstood emotion. If you actually see your spouse in bed with someone else, that's not jealousy- that's anger. No one on earth would accuse you of being deranged for stringing someone up by their heels at that point. In fact, many people have walked free after murdering their spouse *and* the other man or woman, after unexpectedly walking into to clandestine version of "afternoon delight." That's right, even juries recognize that there are just some situations that will push otherwise normal people over the edge.

So, what is jealousy then? In the context we're talking about here, jealously is when you have never seen anything inappropriate between your spouse and someone of the opposite sex, but you feel insecure, anxious, or angry when you know they are in the presence of this person. How does that happen? It requires you to be making pictures or movies in your mind about what they could be doing, and then reacting to your personal mind circus. Again, don't believe it? Try this: grab a small bean bag or something comparable, and then begin tossing it back and forth from one hand to another, and as you continue doing so, start reciting the multiplication tables out loud. If you can access and maintain jealous feelings while doing this, please get in touch with me- the Guinness Book of World Records is always looking for neurological anomalies.

The "Reality Principle" makes it impossible to engage in the needed nonsense that normally allows you to get cranked up and jealous. Emotional experiences that are the result of something that comes from the outside world are feelings. Conversely, an emotional experience born out of memory or that which is in our mind is called *pre-feeling*. You and I, and everyone else in the world, will enjoy life, or not, to the degree that we can keep from mixing these two. The "Reality Principle" says this: whenever you are receiving ample input from the outside world, it will override and dominate any would be input from your inside world.

When does your mind wonder the most? Isn't it when you are

on a long drive, or when you are tossing and turning in bed, unable to sleep? Let me ask you though, when was the last time you were driving in heavy traffic during a downpour of rain and experiencing jealous feelings? Again, unless you are one of those who will be contacting me for entry into the Guinness Book of World Records- *It's never happened.* In a situation like the driving example, there is simply too much external input to for this "mind garbage" to have a snow ball's chance in hell.

How many things do you "know" to be true? Things that you are certain are causing problems in your life or your relationship?

If you're anything like me, you've been *sure* of all kinds of things that turned out to be wrong. Have you ever "known" that if someone else would change their behavior that you would be happy? It's like a punch in the gut when they change, but you still feel the same. Or, have you ever "known" that the reason someone was ignoring you was because they didn't like you, only to discover later that they were just shy, and were thrilled to visit with you when you made the first move?

Truth is, in a situation such as this, we were wrong the entire time, but we rarely try to validate/invalidate our feelings, even, and especially when they are causing us to feel poorly. That's the first step: Start asking "How do I know for sure?"

Whenever you are upset about something you "know" to be true, ask yourself "How do I know for sure?" Then, keep asking that question of any answer you come up with.

Example:

Suppose you are thinking:
"My mother doesn't come visit anymore because of the way my spouse acts."
Ask: How do I know for sure? Response: Well, I can tell by the tension in her voice when I talk to her on the phone.
Ask: How do I know for sure that's what it's about? Response: Well, it couldn't be about anything else.
Ask: How do I know for sure? Response: I guess I don't.

You get the point. Asking "How do I know?" repeatedly, makes you slow down, and notice just how much you really assume in life. If you think your mother doesn't come over for the reason you suspect-

ASK! If it is, *then* you can address it. However, if you are wrong, think of the resentment you'll create in others by never taking the time to verify your self-generated motion pictures.

  Take 7 days, and commit to asking "How do I know?" about anything you "know" that is causing you grief. I think you'll like what you discover.

CHAPTER 36:

THE REAL REASON WHY YOU DON'T BELCH IN CHURCH

"Manners are the hypocrisy of a nation."

-Honore de Balzac

Visionary and pioneer of personal development audio recordings, Earl Nightingale, once said "In the absence of a good role model, simply observe what everyone else is doing-and don't do that!" Vernon Howard, author of several wonderful books on the power of the human mind/spirit wrote "The Truer the Fewer."

My wife and I have a code sound that we utter to each other when we have witnessed someone engaging in "flock" or "herd" behavior; we make the "baah" sound usually herd from sheep. It's a constant reminder for us to spend less time going with what happens to be popular and to think more and more for ourselves.

Kevin Hogan has written that a large part of what we do has very little to do with our values, and almost everything to do with what we think the values of those around us happen to be. This recently came up in a conversation I had with a good friend of mine. I told him that I bet the average convenience store total, when a man buys a Playboy magazine, is probably around twenty to thirty dollars. He immediately started laughing in a way that confirmed he knew exactly what I was talking about.

I remember all too well, walking into a convenience store as a sixteen year old kid, wanting only one thing- the latest issue of Playboy. No one wanted to be standing at the counter, appearing only to have come in for the magazine, without something to hide the Playboy magazine underneath. This was just in case someone we ran into someone we knew, whose values did not find such smut appropriate. Therefore, I'd buy a 32 oz coke, bag of chips, and the Kansas City Star newspaper, which was great for suddenly covering the lovely lady on the cover that vividly flashed PLAYBOY. I didn't know that the majority of the people I worried about were engaging in the very behaviors that I thought would make their eyes pop out of their head. I would later discover that, they too, were using various measures to conceal their choice of magazine at the checkout counter.

What have you avoided, not because it violated your values, but because you were afraid it might violate someone else's?

Many people fall into the trap of thinking they are following their own path, when all they are really doing is polarizing *against* something. I was the poster child for this vicious cycle from my teens through much of my 20's. I shudder to think about the number of things I did for no other reason than to NOT do what someone told me I should do.

It's important to develop an awareness of the distinction between doing what you really want, and doing something only to *not* do what someone else wants. The first will generally lead to feelings of freedom and pleasure; the second will cause you to resent not only others, but yourself as well.

Here's the test:

Ask yourself " If I was suddenly the only person left alive, and could do anything I wanted to, knowing that no one else would ever know what I chose, would I still choose this path?"

If you are only engaging in some action or behavior because you don't want to give someone the pleasure of having watched you follow their suggestion, the above question will likely flush it out. If you find that you would still want to engage in that behavior, but feel a bit of hesitation and have not yet started, you may need to ask another version of that question.

Suppose you want to do X, but are afraid that someone else in your life might not approve of X. The question is: "If I knew that the people I'm thinking about regarding this decision approved, or did it themselves, would I do so without hesitation?"

I once heard a well known speaker tell the story about one of his friends suddenly realizing at the age of 13, that they had simply been following the herd. She told of how she had always eaten her hamburger with ketchup only. No pickles, onions, cheese, mustard, mayonnaise- nothing but meat, bun, and ketchup. One day she thought "Whose hamburger is this?" She was eating her hamburger exactly like her mother always did, and because she had such a close relationship with her mother, she was unconsciously eating, not to enjoy her food, but eating not to offend her mother by being different.

Do you decide what you are going to do, wondering whether or not it makes sense? Does playing it safe leave you feeling passionate about life? I'm not talking about doing things less than legal or ethical. I remember going through a divorce, and for a period of time having $900, a borrowed car, and a cheesy apartment on the wrong side of the tracks until things were settled. What did I do? I took $700 of my $900 and flew to San Juan, Puerto Rico for a week.

When I got back home, I temporarily took a position as a nurse in a correctional facility. I'll never forget being told of my father's comments "I don't know what he's thinking- he can't afford to go to Puerto Rico." My only thoughts were "I must have been able to- because I did." All those years ago, now, and I still think back on that trip as a relaxing, mind freeing experience, one that I'll never forget. From a strictly financial perspective it didn't make sense. But let me suggest to you that making your decisions from purely financial perspectives is a sure way to find yourself on your death bed with a ton of regret.

The time I spent on the oncology floor at the San Diego Naval Hospital, holding the hands of several people in their last hours here on earth taught me one very important thing: People do not regret the mistakes they made, or the things that they did. People wept of the regret they felt about what they *didn't* do. The trips they *never* took; the things they *didn't* say; the hobbies they *didn't* pursue; the crazy things they thought about doing- but *didn't*.

If someone approached me today, and offered me $25,000 if they could strip my mind of the memory of that trip to Puerto Rico- the one I took for $700- I'd say "No, thank you!" Experiences are yours forever.

Chapter 37:

Why Time Goes Faster Each Year

"The secret of life is to enjoy the passage of time."

-James Taylor

It only seems like a year or two ago that I was sitting on the beach in the humid night air of Guam on New Year's Eve, bringing in the new millennium. Have you ever wondered why time seems to go by so much faster each year?

I have my own insights that I would like to share with you. Not only do they offer a plausible explanation for this phenomenon, but they also alerts us to the fact that we don't have as much "time" as we think, no matter how much longer we may live.

Remember when you were a kid coming home from your last day of school, excitedly looking forward to your summer break? Isn't it true that the summers seemed to last forever? And, do you remember how *long* the school year lasted in grade school? What about now though? Don't you find that the summers now seem to go by in a blur?

When you were 10 years old, 1 year represented 1/10, or 10% of your entire life. If you are 50 years old now, that same year represents only 1/50th, or 2% of your life. Because of this, from your perspective of subjective experience (which, I would argue, for most people *is* their experience) a year seems only 1/5 as long as it did at the age of 10.

What does this mean if we apply this formula to various periods of our life?

When you were 6 years old, a year seemed like three years, thus, a nine week summer vacation seemed like 27 weeks!

Now, and I warn you, hang onto your wig for this one, how many times have you heard someone say life starts after 40, 50, or 65? Now that you have a formula for how you experience time, and how much you can expect the passage of time to speed up with each passing year, you come face to face with a very somber, yet potentially motivating fact: At the age of 65 you have only 5 % of your life left, in terms of how you will experience time!

I don't care if you are 18 years old, and haven't even graduated high school yet; you better go ahead and retire NOW!

I can hear some of you now, "What do you mean retire? I have only just started my career!"

I watched my father trudge off to work at 4:30 am each morning, coming home at 3:30 pm, coming home angry, upset and frustrated by a job he hated. I do not remember ever hearing my father say anything good about his job, never.

When I was in my senior year of high school in 1984, I made the comment that I was going to go to work in the same factory where he worked when I graduated. His comment? He said point blank "If they put you to work for me, I'll fire you!" As I look back now, that was the only way he had to communicate to me the contempt he had for his job, and did not want his son to fall into the same trap. I am thankful for the fact that I did not have to go hungry when I was growing up; I never had to worry about having school clothes or healthcare. I always knew I would have a roof over my head. Because of his commitment to providing for his family, I never had to worry about whether I'd have the basic things I needed. However, the stress and pressure my father was feeling at work often made things tense at home. Why wouldn't it? Do they teach you how to deal with your emotions and workplace or family stress in high school? Of course not. Instead we are forced to learn how to work the wonderful algebraic computations that 99% of us have never needed since leaving high school. In short, my father endured nearly 40 years at a place of work he dreaded driving to each day, so he could provide for his family and then relax for the last 5 to 7% of his perceptual life.

I offer this suggestion for the coming year: STOP thinking about the things you can do when you retire, or how you'll be able to get into a hobby or do something you enjoy when you no longer have to work for a living. Make the decision today, that if you are not currently making a living doing something you enjoy, that you are going to do so in by the end of the coming year, or as soon as humanly possible.

I know, I know, someone will write and say "You don't get it! I don't have a choice; I have a family, bills, a house payment, and no education. I do what I do because I have to." I have a good friend who would say "Go tell that to someone else!" I would tell you "Go tell that to the thousands of immigrants that have come to this country with NOTHING-absolutely nothing, and have gone on to become prosperous business men and women.

When I lived in San Diego, my wife used to get her manicure's done at a nail salon owned by a Vietnamese family; a family that lived in a two million dollar home just six blocks from where we lived. Their story was inspiring to say the least. They had come here from Vietnam (all seven of them) with little more than the clothes on their back and a few hundred dollars. They rented the space they continue to use now as the nail salon, and all seven of them slept in the back room on the floor for two years. During this time, they were earning and reinvesting all of their earnings into the business. Today they live a very luxurious life and business is booming.

Fortunately, my father did not have to fire me; after working for a year in a rather relaxed and easy job at the same factory where he worked, I quit. Not because the work was hard, or the pay was terrible, I quit because I watched 600 people march in to the time clock each day, talking about how forward they looked to the day they could retire. That was in 1984. In recent years, I have attended the funerals of many of the men I had once worked with, who had finally reached retirement age, and then died less than five years after retiring.

Time *does* seem like it moves faster, and will continue to do so at the rate described above. We don't have near as much time as we think.

So, what would you do if you knew you only had five years left to live? Two years? One? Would you do *anything* different? Whatever your answer, what's stopping you from doing it *now*? There is only one answer: FEAR.

Is this the year that you will overcome your fears and embark on a life that you would be proud of having as an obituary, or, will you continue to, as Thoreau was fond of saying "...lead a life of quiet desperation"?

It's been suggested that there are two kinds of people; those who make plans, and those who make excuses. My intuition is that you are more interested in making plans. Otherwise, you'd be doing something "constructive" like playing video games, instead of reading this book.

The answer for doing anything you want to do exists. The only thing that has ever stopped you is fear; the fear *you create* inside your head, by the images, sounds and feelings you put together. Will you leave that behind this year? I sure hope so.

I am proposing to you, that when you *do something you enjoy for a living*, in a sense, you are already enjoying retirement. However, I'm willing to bet, that when you are living like this, the idea of retirement probably won't even enter your mind. Why would it? No one looks forward to the day they can stop doing something they enjoy! So, how soon are you going to start?

Chapter 38:

Better Not Use *That* Finger

"At some point in time, he made a hand gesture in the direction of the officer with what was believed to be a weapon."

-Ricky Boren

As a professional speaker, a big part of my job is to rapidly create, and then maintain an atmosphere of receptivity in the audience members. One would think that the most powerful tool at the disposal of a professional speaker would be the words they choose- and words are important- but there is something that is far more powerful.

See, the words are generally what people are most conscious of, and what they are paying the most attention to. This is one of many reasons why body language is so incredibly influential. There is so much going on non-verbally, that it's simply too much for people to track consciously. And yet, their unconscious mind is paying very close attention to everything. When was the last time that your eyes slammed shut and your head twisted to the side or jerked backwards, only to determine a second later that a bug was about to fly into your eye? This is but one example of the hyper-alert awareness with which the unconscious mind monitors everything around you.

We've all had the experience of meeting someone and almost instantly getting a "bad vibe." Just as many of us have met someone who minutes later felt like an old trusted friend. What on earth can we know about someone seconds or minutes after meeting them? Very little. But sometimes, that proves to be more than enough.

Let's examine one particular aspect of body language; the gesture of pointing with the index finger when attempting to impress upon someone the importance of what you are talking about, more commonly called "pointing." While using this gesture may empower the speaker and make *them* feel confident, it's one of the quickest ways I know of to generate negative feelings in others. In fact, in one particular experiment, 72 % of the participants rated the speaker using a finger point as negative, finding them aggressive and rude. Furthermore, these same participants later found that they were not able to recall nearly as much of what the speaker had presented as those in the group listening to the speaker when he gave the same presentation without pointing. It would seem, then, that simply pointing at the audience caused them to dislike the speaker and close their mind off to the information he was presenting.

Want to see an example of someone who points at his guests almost every night? Watch the O'Reilly Factor with Bill O'Reilly on Fox News. Bill waves his finger and points directly at the guest when he's trying to drive home his point. Is it effective? I'll let you decide. Just watch and see how you feel as you watch him point at others, and if that feels bad, just multiply that times 10 to understand how it would feel if you were the guest. Hey, I guess since he has a multi-million dollar contract, he can afford to offend people. The question is, can you?

Clearly, using your hands to gesture allows you to communicate more powerfully. Just try giving a presentation with your hands tied and see what happens to your effectiveness as a communicator. So, if pointing with the index finger is a bad idea, how can we punctuate with our hands, making a segment of our message stand out?

Just touch the tip of your index finger and the tip of your thumb together, while leaving the rest of your hand open and relaxed. Anytime you might have used your index finger to point in the past, simply substitute with this gesture.

When audience members in the aforementioned experiment were asked to evaluate the speakers who used the gesture that involves touching the thumb and index finger tips together, they rated the speaker as focused and thoughtful. Do you think that being viewed as "thoughtful" instead of "rude" might be useful with a group of people you wish to influence?

If this is something you would like to immediately incorporate into your communication, the best thing you can do is get in front of a mirror. Play with this new gesture, discovering just how many ways you can use it to eloquently embellish your message.

By doing everything you can to keep the "gate" of their mind open, you will be able to contribute in ways they will come to appreciate immensely. The faster you get comfortable using this gesture, instead of the archaic finger point, the faster you'll find others becoming pleasantly receptive to both you *and* your message.

CHAPTER 39:

THE PAINFULLY HAPPY WAY OF GETTING THINGS DONE

"People often say that motivation doesn't last. Well, neither does bathing–that's why we recommend it daily."

-Zig Ziglar

Millions of magazines are sold each month, simply because of a few words on the cover. The words "Weight Loss Secrets", or something along those lines, compel people to add the magazine to their grocery cart, in hopes that what they have been looking for will be found inside. They are looking for an easy way to lose weight and keep it off.

While I have worked with quite a few men and women that wanted to lose weight over the last 10 years, those who have lost weight and kept it off have done something that those who have not didn't. First, though, I'd like to compare and contrast two hypothetical clients. The first being someone who wants to lose weight; the second client is someone who has been having "panic attacks."

A client who has been having anxious thoughts and feelings, experiences pain and discomfort while this is going on. When they are not experiencing "anxiety" they feel relief. They do not need to discover a compelling reason to become "panic free." Their panicking or "anxiety" is enough discomfort; it is reason enough by itself. This person will take the suggestions that I offer and the exercises that I give them, and they will follow them to the letter. Much like an animal with its foot caught in a trap, they will do *anything* to get free. For this reason, I have never had a client in 10 years that was not able to resolve their "panic disorder" or "anxiety attacks."

Now, let's contrast this with the client that wants to lose weight. They are dissatisfied with the way they look or feel, but not necessarily with the process or behaviors that are responsible for how they look and feel. Namely, they do not dislike eating or sitting on their butt instead of exercising. For most people, the relief they experience comes from *not* doing the behaviors that will help. When they choose to watch T.V. instead of going to the gym, or to eat three slices of cake instead of one, they feel a welcome comfort...for a little while.

Before long, the emotions of guilt, frustration, or anger make their presence known, and back and forth they go. It would seem they are stuck between a rock and a hard place, but closer examination reveals something radically different.

Have you ever known someone who ignored their health for 30, 40, or 50 years, eating what they want, never exercising or getting an annual physical? My guess is that you've also known someone like I've just described, who, after a near fatal heart attack, and upon getting back on their feet, completely changed their behaviors. They now exercise every day, eat only healthy foods and they visit their doctor regularly. What happened?

Pain is an incredible tool for getting someone to take immediate action. It's been said that everyone has their breaking point, and it has been my experience that this breaking point comes when we have hit our pain threshold. Once someone who has experienced a near fatal heart attack has reflected on the pain that others would have felt from their absence, or has experienced the fear of dying, they suddenly find themselves doing what is required to become healthy.

You can't imagine the number of people who have told me "Oh, I already know about the consequences, but I still can't seem to get motivated." They may "know" the consequences, but they haven't *felt* them. Studies using sophisticated eye scanning equipment have shown that when overweight men and women are reading an article that talks about the tragic events that can result from remaining overweight, their eyes skip across that section, and they begin reading again where the text shifts to another, less painful, topic.

HERE'S THE SECRET TO WEIGHT LOSS:

Walk or exercise 7 days a week, at least 30 minutes a day, and with enough intensity to break a sweat, eat healthier foods, and consume fewer calories each day.

AND, HERE'S THE SECRET TO MAKING THAT HAPPEN:

Dip your heart, mind, body and soul into the pain you will experience if you don't.

I don't mean read about it, I mean close your eyes, and vividly imagine your loved one's sobbing uncontrollably at your funeral, or at the side of your hospital bed as you watch from that bed attentively, but unable to move or speak because of the ravages of a stroke. When you can envision these things until *you* are crying, sobbing, or deeply feeling pain, you will have taken the first step in getting enough leverage to change your life for the long haul.

The movie *The Secret* is a great movie. It's hard to watch it without getting a good warm feeling and a sense of inner peace. However, the idea of the "Law of Attraction" has, in some cases, created more confusion and turmoil than anything else. If you are 70 lbs overweight, have high blood pressure, and Type II Diabetes, feeling warm and having a sense of inner peace is going to take you to an early grave. If your goal is simply to feel happy, and you're not particularly concerned about how long you live, or what the quality of those years will be like, then that strategy works. If you *do* want to live a longer and healthier life, however, it's not likely that thinking about being thinner and feeling good about it is going to attract anything other than denial about your current situation.

Sadly, the *The Secret* has spurred many people into thinking that "negative" or painful thoughts are forbidden and are to be pushed away like the plague. To do so, though, is to leave behind the most powerful motivator on earth- PAIN.

Kevin Hogan devised what I consider to be one of the most valuable visualization methods for using pain constructively that I've ever seen. When I say "devised" I mean he's brought it into the public's awareness. It was based on some very recent research on visualization and motivation. It involves split screen imaging.

Imagine for a moment that in front of you is a large 60 inch television. Imagine a line splitting the screen down the middle; on the left side is an image of how you look now, and examples of all of the "bad" or painful things you can expect if you stay this way. On the right side is an image of you looking how you will at your desired healthy weight. With that image, be sure to place all of the benefits of looking and feeling like that "you." The key is to observe them both at the same time.

Why does this work so powerfully? Two words: **cognitive dissonance.** Your brain and nervous system "freaks" when two contrasting images or thoughts are held simultaneously. It is simply too uncomfortable, and therefore, your unconscious has one primary goal at this point; it is focused on resolving the pain. If the image on your left side is painful enough, your brain will do whatever it has to do to bring your reality into alignment with the healthy image on the right side. What will have to happen? You guessed it...exercise and changing eating habits.

In summary, pain is not a "negative" or "positive" thing. It is simply a tool that is appropriate at times, and not so appropriate at others. Harness the power of pain, combine it with the power of pleasure, and find yourself doing the things you always wanted to do.

Chapter 40:

High Self Esteem or Idiot?

"The truest characters of ignorance are vanity, pride and arrogance."

-Samuel Butler

How can you tell if someone has high self-esteem? The best test in the world is to watch how they treat those they need nothing from. How do they treat the waitress, or the gas station attendant, or the bellhop when checking into the hotel?

We are often tricked into thinking that the person with a BIG ego has a high self-esteem. This isn't the case though. In fact, it is impossible to have a BIG ego and high self-esteem at the same time. Let's look at two different scenarios: A. The person without much ego, and low self- esteem. B. The person with a BIG ego, and low self- esteem.

The person lacking much ego and having low self- esteem is likely to take the negative things that happen in life, and direct them inward, blaming themselves. The person with a BIG ego, and a low self-esteem, however, is more likely to blame others, and project their frustration and anger outward. In other words, the things that go wrong in their life will always be someone else's fault.

The more accepting we are of ourselves, the more accepting we are of others. It's hard, bordering on impossible, to be any more accepting of others than we are of ourselves. Many people confuse moods with self- esteem. Moods are very temporary, and serve as a filter through which we view the world at that moment. People with very high self-esteem don't have near as much "sway" in their behavior when they experience changing moods.

On the other hand, those with low self-esteem are more or less driven by their ever changing moods. In short, the quality of the life they experience is all wrapped up in their moods.

There may be times when people don't feel like doing a task they had earlier promised a good friend they would do. People with low self-esteem will let the mood of "not feeling like it right now" justify not completing the task. Meanwhile, the person with high self-esteem will do it anyway, even though their mood is not conducive. The message is short, but oh so powerful: To make lasting changes in your external world, and to enjoy the experience of life, it is essential to work on the inside, to build a strong self-esteem.

What's one big contribution you can make in this area? The key is to accept yourself as you currently are now.

As strange as it seems, the longer you reject the things you don't like about yourself, the longer they will persist. The instant you accept the things you have not liked about yourself, they quickly start melting away. If you find yourself thinking that the information in this chapter contradicts the information in the last chapter, use this as an opportunity to begin thinking in terms of this *and* that, instead of this *or* that.

CHAPTER 41:

TRAVELS THROUGH THE STATE OF CONFUSION

"Advertising is 85% confusion and 15% commission."

-Fred Allen

In the age of instant communication, many of us have found ourselves being jerked around like puppets on a string. We respond to every ringing phone, "Instant Message" and just about every other form of the "stop whatever you are doing and talk to me now" demands that come our way.

The result is predictable. A day filled with the stop-start-stop-start pattern almost always leaves you vulnerable to what Zig Ziglar has often referred to as confusing activity with accomplishment.

This is what happens, when, at the end of the day, we look back and realize that we have been extremely busy, and yet, when we examine our accomplishments, we're shocked to discover that nothing important got done.

Just a few years ago, it was an honor to be able to say "Yes!" when someone asked if you were able to multi-task. Multi-tasking was the new buzzword that described something that took several years for many to catch on to.

Today, almost everyone understands that multi-tasking was a concept of necessity; downsizing and cutbacks required one person to do the work of three. Clearly, it would not have worked out so well, if we would have gone to an employee and told them "Hey, you now have to do both your work *and* the work that Dave used to do, and we're going to pay you less than we did when all you did was your work."

Instead, people were told "We've noticed that you are a marvelous multi-tasker" As attention starved as most people are, when someone told them they had noticed their "rare" and important skill (multi-tasking), they felt good about it. Men and women everywhere felt good…for a little while. Over time it became painfully obvious that they had been sold a bill of goods that didn't measure up.

The research in this area is conclusive: Multi-tasking does not increase efficiency, and in most cases, only slows down and "gums" up most any process. However, millions of people have not stayed current with the research in this area. They still hold the belief that those who can multi-task can get more done, and have established some "bad" habits when it comes to getting, and then staying focused.

Anytime we are moving through the day in a scattered manner, it almost always comes down to the fact that we are not clear about our priorities. If most people would stop several times each day to ask themselves "Why am I doing what I'm doing right now?" they'd most likely be surprised at how often the real reason involved *not* having to do something else. Many "important" activities are nothing more than an escape mechanism; one that serves to distract us from what's really important.

When we don't know why we are doing what we are, the possibility exists that we are simply doing something pleasurable to avoid doing something we deem uncomfortable. Is it any wonder, then, that we so quickly answer every ringing phone? This provides us with one more distraction from the thing we are trying to avoid.

Think about it; how many times each year after January 1st, have you done something like clean the garage, to avoid having to do your taxes? Normally, cleaning the garage wouldn't bring much pleasure. However, when contrasted with a "tax" day, it suddenly becomes an enjoyable endeavor. So, establishing your priorities for the day is the first step. Only after you have determined what *is* important can you gain an instant awareness of what *isn't*.

On April 7th of 2008, I was having breakfast with my mother. It had been scheduled the week before and was therefore on my schedule as a priority that day.

I had forgotten to turn off my cell phone, and had set it earlier to "vibrate." When my receptionist sent a text to my phone, my phone started buzzing against the table top, indicating that I had received a message. When I picked up my phone to turn it off, I could see that I had received a call from Kim Agle, the producer of Fox and Friend's at Fox News. She was calling to see if I was available for a live interview on national television at 3:30 pm. I would be analyzing the body language of President Bush and John McCain.

You might be thinking "Vince, you did drop everything right then and call her back immediately, right?" No, I didn't.

The short time I had scheduled with my mother that morning still had about 15 minutes remaining. Since I had failed to silence the message until I was ready for it, I was faced with making a decision about what to do. Hard? Not at all. I was very clear about my priority at that moment. In the 15 minutes I had waited, Kim had found someone else to do the interview. When I finally spoke to her, she said "Is it okay if we call again Vince, is that okay?" I said "Sure, I'd love to hear from you again."

In terms of free publicity, and the resulting speaking engagements and product sales, a few minutes of airtime on Fox News is ultimately worth several thousand dollars. The real cost, however, is found in deviating from your values, from your pre-determined priorities, and getting in the habit of jumping midstream from one thing to another. My mother is 63 years old. The day will come, when I would trade everything I have for another 15 minutes with her. I'll take it now instead.

Would I love for Kim to call again? Certainly. But please understand, there are very few phone calls, that, if not answered immediately, will ruin the rest of your life.

Get rid of "call waiting." If you were standing outside your office talking with someone, and then, someone else walked up and started tapping on your shoulder, wanting to talk to you about something, would you stop and visit with them, making the person you had been talking to wait? Why then, would you flash over to take an incoming call while talking to someone else?

Get a secretary or an answering service to take *all* of your calls. I can't begin to tell you how freeing it was to hire someone to take *all* of my incoming business calls. If you are answering your own calls, I'll bet a dollar to a doughnut that you are neglecting an important area of your life, wasting time and attention, fielding calls here and there, while you could be working to promote your business, or spending time with your family.

In short, determine what your priorities for the next day will be. Then, once you have started working on one, refuse to be distracted by anything less than a true emergency until you are through. I once heard someone suggest that you can only say "No" and smile, when you have a much bigger "Yes" burning inside.

Your "Yes" can only burn when you know what your priorities are and can then maintain that awareness. By contrast, the insignificance of the other things that come up will be evident, and easy to say "No" to.

CHAPTER 42:

EXPLOIT YOUR STRENGTHS AND IGNORE YOUR WEAKNESSES

"Strength does not come from physical capacity. It comes from indomitable will."

-Mahatma Ganhdi

I have to admit, I was caught up in the "fix my weaknesses" mindset at one time. Sound's logical, does it not? While your "weaknesses" will certainly have to be addressed if they are significant enough, far too often, that's just not the case. More often than not, what's really holding someone back has more to do with them not focusing on their strengths; they are not maximizing the power they already have, and are instead, focusing on bringing the weaker aspects of themselves up to par.

The fact of the matter is this: Most people excel at a handful of things, and border on pathetic in far more areas.

I am an idiot when it comes to mechanical things. When my bathtub is leaking I call a plumber. If the computer starts getting goofy, I call a computer tech. Car needs worked on? "Hello, Mr. Good wrench please." You get the picture.

My strengths are in presenting, training, teaching and consulting. All things that involve speaking and talking to other people. I took to this area like a duck to water, and have invested hundreds of hours and thousands of dollars in continually getting even stronger in this area. Have you ever met someone who was determined to be good at everything they do? Determined as they may be, there is one factor that makes this an ill-formed goal: *Time*

The one thing we all have the same amount of, whether it's Bill Gates, or a homeless person sleeping on the streets, is the amount of time we have available. We each have 24 hours each day, and, we either use it wisely, or not.

With very few exceptions, those who are living a life that is close to, or even exceeds the life they always dreamed of, have identified their strengths and the things they thoroughly enjoy doing, and have then focused most of their time and energy there. They have mastered the use of *The Pareto Principle*, or the 80/20 Rule. This rule states that 80% of the results you create come from just 20 % of the activities or things you do.

While it may vary a bit (90/10, 70/30) it's pretty darn close just with about anything you apply it to. 80% of the world's wealth is owned by 20 % of the people. 80% of the crime is committed by 20% of the criminals. 80% of any stock portfolio's profits come from 20% of the stocks.

Key Point:

Since 80% of your results come from 20% of the things you do, find out what those things are, and do *more* of those, and *less* of everything else. The things that you feel like you aren't very good at, are probably not part of the 20% of the things you do that account for 80% of the results. Therefore, in the grand scheme of things they really don't matter that much.

More than anything else, perhaps, our weak areas work on our ego. Most people aren't comfortable with not being good at something. I no longer feel anything less than comfortable about the areas where I don't excel. Besides, why would I want to take time away from the things I enjoy doing, the things I'm good at, when for $7-$30 an hour, there is someone that does excel at what I need done, that can do it in a fraction of the time, and do it right?

If you will spend the coming year identifying what you are good at, and squeezing all you can out of that, by focusing more of your time in that area, the results you create will be so significant that you'll finally see your weaknesses for what they are.

Does that mean you have to let go completely of becoming stronger in the weaker areas? Of course not. Just make sure that you are spending most of your time on the 20% that accounts for 80% of your results.

CHAPTER 43:

DID EARL NIGHTINGALE KNOW ABOUT THE RAS?

"The most important thing about goals is having one."

-Albert F. Geoffrey

It would be hard to make it to the age of ten without having someone tell you about the power of a goal. Yet, as I travel around this orb we live on, I'm always amazed at the number of people who are pushing forward with all of their strength and coming up empty handed.

Each week I get to speak to everyone from high ranking officers in the military and CEO's of well known companies, to the men and women who are currently between jobs, or who are just getting ready to enter the market place. Whether I'm presenting in New York, Michigan, or North Carolina, one of the most common challenges I see people dealing with, is the result of not having a crystal clear goal.

In short, show me someone with such a vivid description of what they want to be experiencing one month, one year, or five years from now, that it has become hard to not think about it, and I'll show you someone that will bypass those with more education, money, talent, looks or friends in high places.

Many years ago, Earl Nightingale spoke about this phenomenon in his classic recording *The Strangest Secret.*

What was this strange secret?

We become what we think about most of the time.

If this is true, *why* is it true? What causes this to happen?
To avoid getting into a week long discussion of neurology, I'll

simply tell you about the Reticular Activating System (RAS). I should tell you that this is not something you have to run out and spend $1500 on. In fact, there is no amount of money you could invest that would afford you a device that would do anything close to the RAS. You see, you already have an RAS in place. That's right. This is the neurological structure that serves as a filter, or screening device of sorts, making certain things virtually impossible not to notice, and effectively blocking other things from ever reaching your conscious awareness.

Remember the last time you bought a new vehicle? Isn't it true that you immediately started to see that same vehicle, in the very same color, everywhere you went? This had nothing to do with the number of them on the road; they had always been there. Now that *you* have this vehicle, it has suddenly become relevant to you. This causes your RAS to change its filters. It now searches for, and highlights, any match it finds, thrusting its discovery into your consciousness. It happens with clothes, cars, glasses, hairstyles, you name it.

If an optometrist is watching a play, he or she will notice the different eye glass styles of the other people in the audience. A jeweler will notice the rings, watches, necklaces and broaches. The optometrist may not even notice that someone is wearing a watch; the jeweler may not even notice they are wearing glasses. The RAS is a magnificent system indeed.

A clearly written goal has the power to turn your RAS on high power. You may be wondering what in the world your RAS has to do with goal setting. That's very simple. Your RAS will allow you to notice the elements of your experience that will enable you to achieve any goal on earth.

You hear some people say things like "there are lots of opportunities right now" or, maybe they take the opposite view of "right now opportunities are scarce." There is never a time when there are any more or any less opportunities. There are simply times that you have been prepared to notice them, and times when others could see them, but you couldn't. Why? You guessed it, your RAS.

The moment you put a pen to paper and start crafting your goal, you begin tweaking your RAS. You literally change what it detects and what it deletes, by determining what is important to you and what isn't. Wanting something is not enough. Until you have written it out in detail, describing it until it begins to crystallize and take on a life of its own, you simply will not be able to provide your brain with enough high quality information to turn the scanning beam of your RAS on with full force.

For years, I wanted to earn a living speaking, and I really wanted it. However, it wasn't until I committed my thoughts to writing that things started happening. After having presented a blueprint of what I wanted to my mind, my RAS began to notice the people, places, and situations that would be needed to make my goal come alive. It's important to note, that there were no more opportunities for me at that time than at any other time in my life. They had always been there. The *big* difference was that now I was noticing them. And *that* is the difference that makes the difference.

It's been said that we should "start with the end in mind." What's that mean? Pretend you have already accomplished your goal. You are looking at it from the perspective of it already being done. As you imagine looking at your situation, having achieved your goal, what does the outcome look like? Sound like? Smell like? Feel like? Taste like? Describe your goal in such detail (by writing it down) that its initial ambiguity turns into a crystal clear picture.

Think of it like this. If you want to write with precision, pretend you are tasked with writing a set of instructions for someone to follow so they could rescue a child from a cave, and the cave holds only a limited amount of oxygen. I'm betting you wouldn't leave anything fuzzy. You would write with such precision that there was no possibility of them getting to the wrong cave, or taking the wrong path in the right cave. When you write with this much clarity when writing your own goals, I warn you, you better hang on, because your life will begin moving rapidly in the new desired direction.

CHAPTER 44:

USING THE BRAIN OF A WAITER TO GET AHEAD

"Happiness? That's nothing more than health and a poor memory."

-Albert Schweitzer

Have you ever had the experience of having the day off, a chance to unwind and relax, and yet, your mind was gnawing at you the whole time?

One reason for this is that most people have a great deal of "unfinished business" hanging around. If you have ever started something, but then had to place it on the back burner while you move on to something else, then you know exactly what I'm talking about.

Back burner or not, the "out of sight out of mind" theory does not hold water here. When a task is not complete, it will amplify the feelings of stress and tension you feel as you move through the day doing other things.

Russian psychologist Bluma Zeigarnik made a discovery that explains why this occurs. He noticed that waiters remembered in great detail the orders that were pending; the ones that had not yet been served.

However, as soon as they had placed the meal on the table, the waiters immediately forgot what had been ordered. What has now been termed as the Zeigarnik Effect, explains why unfinished business can literally wear us down, sending us into overwhelm.

The Zeigarnik Effect creates a "psychic tension" to drive us to complete an action. Once the waiter had placed the plate on the table, it was a finished project, and the mind discharged that information as it was no longer relevant. This "release" cleared conscious space for other things.

What is vitally important to remember, however, is that we only have so many chunks of conscious space available. When we overload consciousness, we begin to feel stressed and confused.

Many physical manifestations of illness may also be the result of "unfinished business." Certain emotional or psychological experiences that were not effectively dealt with at the time can cause problems long after the event has passed.

Cardiologists often refer to what is known as the "Anniversary Effect"- the tendency for people to return on or around the date of what just happens to be the anniversary date of a traumatic experience in their past. In order to restore and maintain balance, we must increase our capacity for health.

As we start to close open loops, by finishing unfinished business, we start to see our health making positive turns. This may involve working through the list of actual projects we have opened, that are *still* open, far longer than they should have been, or effectively dealing the psychological junk from something that was not handled adequately at the time.

While we cannot change the past, we can change the manner in which we have been responding consciously, unconsciously, or both, to that event.

CHAPTER 45:

ARE YOU DOING THE RIGHT THINGS, OR JUST DOING THINGS RIGHT?

"People, like nails, lose their effectiveness when they lose direction and begin to bend."

-Walter Savage Landor

Successful people have the habit of doing the things that "failures" won't do. They don't like doing them either, necessarily, but their disliking is subordinated to the strength of their purpose. This is not a strategy used by the masses, however. Far too many whine and complain about their lives, refusing to do anything to change their experience. However, successful people have the ability to focus on doing the *right things*, and this, makes all the difference in the world.

On the other end of the spectrum we have the perfectionist. These are the people who are focused on *doing things right*, rather than on doing the right things. They get hung up on the details; the details of the wrong things.

If you climb to the top of a ladder that is against the wrong wall, you are simply at the top of a ladder that is leaning against the wrong wall. Clearly, it is better to be on the *second* rung of the ladder that is leaning against the *right* wall, than at the *top* of the ladder leaning against the *wrong* one.

When people are telling me about their "lack" of time, and how stressed their life is because they just can't get the things they need to get done wrapped up, or how "busy" and overwhelmed they are, I always listen closely to what follows. After they are through talking "business", and they start to chit chat about life in general, I almost always hear the self-imposed obstacles to their progress.

When someone can tell me about the personal life of the contestants on American Idol, or give me the inning by inning, play by play scoop on last night's baseball game, I know I have someone before me that, truly, cannot see the forest for the trees. My company commander in boot camp had one standard reply when someone used the "I didn't have time" excuse when asked why they didn't get something done. He would simply ask, "Did you sleep last night?" Of course, the answer was always "Yes." He would scream "Then you had time!"

The sad fact is this: Most people simply are not willing to pay the price for the things they say they want. Do you realize that we all have to either pay the price of discipline, or the pain of regret?

The things that matter, the things that will really count towards the achievement of your goals, will most likely be at odds with the way the rest of the world lives. When you begin to use a part of each of your days off to work on things that will help you achieve one or more of your goals, many people just won't get it. Most people hate their jobs so much, that all they can think about is anything *except* work related activities. If this is your situation, let that be the first indication that you are not following your heart, or engaged in the profession where you can contribute the most.

When you start to write articles, read, listen to audio programs, or practice and prepare for the next day's sale instead of going to the bar, some people will think you have lost your mind. Why? You are an uncomfortable reminder to them, of just how much of their time, and how much of their life is wasted on nonsense.

For a number of years I drank heavily, and my life was continually spinning out of control. Then, one of my early mentors told me that if a person would read only ten minutes a day on one particular topic, that in five years they would be in the top 2% of experts in that field. I took that to heart, but I cheated a little. I decided to read at least an hour each day, and as a result, I am an expert in each of the subjects I write about and teach. It's really as simple as that.

The realization came to me one day as I was driving by a bar that I had frequented at that time. I saw the very same people pull in to that bar after work, day in, and day out. They would sit and drink for 2, 3 or 4 hours a night before finally creeping home. I asked myself "What would they experience in their lives if they would take just one hour of that time each night and read, listen to audio programs, and *do* things that contributed to the accomplishment of their goals?" The answer was obvious.

I made the decision that day that I would never again waste the most precious gift any of us are ever given- TIME- by sitting in a bar with the equivalent of rudderless ships lost at sea all around me. Instead, I became a recluse of sorts, choosing to spend my time alone doing productive things, venturing out to mingle with others only after I had identified that they had a positive direction in their lives, and were working on it daily. As you might imagine, that limits the number of people there are to hang out with, and you wind up having to cut several people loose, but that is a decision that changed my life, and I have never looked back or had even one second of regret.

Chances are very good, that if you have been frequently saying "I just don't have enough time to exercise, read, or write" that the real problem is not to be found in a lack of time, but in the lack of clearly defined priorities and clarity about what is important to you. In other words, you are probably wasting a great deal of time doing things that are pleasant, and that you enjoy, rather on getting to the things that matter.

Decide today, that before you ever again complain about not having enough time to do the things that matter the most, that you will first take a brutally honest look at how much time you are wasting doing things that you may very well enjoy, but that have absolutely no payoff other than the escape they provide from doing the things that will move you to the next level.

CHAPTER 46:

WHAT DOES YOUR LIFE MEAN?

"Your life's meaning is the difference that it makes. If it doesn't make a difference, it has no meaning."

-Lyndon Duke

Lyndon Duke is best known for his studies on the linguistics of suicide. Duke felt that if you could understand suicide, you would also have developed an understanding for all human unhappiness.

Duke once suggested that when we are on our death bed, we will be asking "What's different? What is different on this planet because I was here?" If nothing is different, then you didn't make a difference. If you didn't make a difference, then your life had no meaning. What doesn't make a difference has no meaning.

Lyndon had experienced exceptional success early in his life. Later, after a series of events, he had hit rock bottom. One day, as he lay face down on his living room floor, he heard his neighbor mowing the yard. Above the sound of the growling lawnmower, he also heard the voice of his neighbor, the man pushing the lawn mower. His neighbor was singing as he mowed the yard.

In a flash, Duke realized what he wanted more than anything else. He wanted to experience a life so simple that he could mow the yard and sing at the same time. His new goal was to simply become an average person.

He started to think about the possibility of having a simple and comfortable life. This is a man who had been a highly intellectual university professor. Lyndon decided that he wanted to become an average person, enjoying an average life. Eventually, he came to the understanding that one's life did not have to be exceptional, and that an average person, living an average life every day, could make a big difference. Thus, an average person could have a life full of meaning.

Remember, Duke defined meaning as the difference that you make. Lyndon Duke made the differences he was able to make, and didn't get frustrated about the differences he would like to make, but couldn't.

Duke knew something that many never figure out: It's easier to do those things we practice or do frequently. If we want the process of making a difference to be easier, we can do so by simply making a point to consistently make a difference. Sounds embarrassingly simple, but in truth, it's really as simple as that. Humans will find the things they do frequently, easier to do. This includes accessing the less desired states and emotions like misery and frustration. If we "practice" being miserable and frustrated, we will get more proficient at being miserable and frustrated.

After having mastered becoming average, Duke suggested that others who were interested simply get up each morning, willing to live out another average day.

While studying those who had taken their own life, and looking at what he called the linguistics of suicide (studying their suicide notes), he discovered that the people who had taken their own lives, had the unrealistic expectation that every day, every moment, every event, had to be the most spectacular ever. If it wasn't, it meant (to them) that something was wrong. Those who committed suicide had navigated their way through life with a rigid set of "rules" about what constitutes a good day. The rigidity of these inflexible rules made having a "good day" all but it impossible. Over time, these people came to believe that they were deficient somehow.

Many of the things you would rather *not* experience in your life *will* happen. People you love will die or get sick. Things will break. Earthquakes, floods and hurricanes or tornados will continue to "decorate" the landscape and claim innocent lives in the process. However, when you acknowledge and accept this ahead of time, when those things do happen, your ability to recover or bounce back is enhanced tremendously.

What would it be like for you to experience a series of happy average days? The next time you are convinced you are having a terrible

day, ask yourself what you are comparing it to, or what rules you are using for that particular situation and what would have to happen for you
to call it "fun" or "successful".

Make it easy to have great days, and difficult to have "bad" days.
Most people have it set up the other way around!

CHAPTER 47:

THE COCKTAIL PARTY FACTOR

"Insecurity is just something that's there all the time. I've never been crippled by it."

-Catherine Keener

I'll never forget my experience with a woman who had booked an appointment with me after telling me she had "no self-esteem!" After I had asked her a few questions, playfully expressing doubt about her low self- esteem, so I could gauge her response, she firmly stated "I *know* I have no self-esteem, because every time I walk into a room, I just know that everyone is talking about me!" "Wow, that's really arrogant and self-centered" I quipped. This had the intended effect of jolting her out of her usual pattern of behavior.

"Mary, have you ever considered that maybe, everyone else is so busy worrying that people are talking about them, that they don't have time to be thinking much about you?" I asked. I continued "If there is one thing I have learned, both through my work with hundreds of people, and the awareness of my own tendencies, it's that we all, at some point and time in our lives, suffer from what I call the 'cocktail party' phenomenon."

Her attention was riveted on me as I explained the *cocktail party factor.* "Mary, most men and women, when walking into a cocktail party, are convinced that as they enter the room, that everyone else is interrupting their previous train of thought, to focus exclusively on them. If and when this does happen, they are only focusing on us long enough to worry about what we might be thinking about them." Then, I gave Mary an exercise designed get her *out* of her own head, and to shift her attention to the *outside* world.

I had her close her eyes and pretend that as she walked into a room, she could see the thoughts people were having in an imaginary cartoon bubble above their head. I had her think of people while "seeing" thought bubbles containing such words as "They probably know this jewelry isn't real" or "I think she can tell I've had a hair transplant."

A few weeks later, she reported back, telling me that while it had been great fun and such a release at first, she quickly tired of the activity and had simply gone about the business of thinking about her own purpose for entering a room of people. If she had gone in to make a new friend, then that's what she did. If she had gone in to find a key contact and obtain some key information for her latest venture, that's what she did.

No longer was she wasting valuable time, fretting about what others might be thinking of her. And, on the rare occasion that she started to worry, she'd instantly zero in on the "thought bubbles" of others, and find herself giggling inside seconds later.

How much more would you get done, and how much more expressive would you be, if you didn't let the thoughts of what others might think crop up during the creative stages of your project?

Clearly, considering the perspective of others can be extremely useful in the later stages of a project. However, internal editing based on our hallucinations of what our peers or co-workers might think, can only serve to stifle our creativity and lead us to produce another mediocre piece of work at best.

Unfettered thinking and brainstorming can, and does, lead to insightful breakthroughs and advances in virtually every known field. Can you imagine the delay in the light by which you are reading this now, if Thomas Edison would have been concerned about what everyone else might have thought? Not too long ago, some felt that anyone who promoted the idea of a man walking on the moon was a bit wacky; they were "lunatics" and were lacking mental stability. I'm sure Neil Armstrong is glad that NASA didn't concern itself with what these naysayers might have thought about their space adventures.

By the way, there are *some* people who will spend a lot of time thinking or talking about others. This comes in the form of gossip and "back biting" and is generally meant to somehow undermine the intended target of the unfounded criticism or slander. You may not have realized one very important psychological component of this situation;

when someone is publically talking about someone behind their back; it's the equivalent of having a spotlight shining on them, while wearing a banner that says "I'm very insecure and uncertain of myself. I talk about others in an attempt to divert attention away from me, hoping they won't notice *my* weaknesses."

What would it be like to feel your ideas flowing effortlessly? How many projects have you finished, knowing in your heart that you had much better "stuff" buried inside, "stuff" that you chose to leave buried because of how silly someone might find one or more of your ideas? Resolve to STOP this nonsense now, and start expressing your strengths. You can always edit later. But first, just get it out!

Key Point:

Realize that your thoughts about what others might think, will act as a vice that clamps down on your stream of creativity. Understand that no one is thinking about you as much as you think, and if they are, this only serves as proof that they are insecure and not as relevant as you might have previously thought.

CHAPTER 48:

BE A "PEN" HEAD AND CHOOSE YOUR FRIENDS WISELY

"The tartness of his face sours ripe grapes."

-William Shakespeare

Let me give you a quick example of how rapidly and easily you can change what you're feeling, by simply making some changes in what you do with your face.

Place a pen or a pencil in your mouth, holding it on each end with your fingers, keeping it horizontal to your face. Push it as far back between your upper and lower teeth as you can so that it pulls the corners of your mouth tight. Then, just bite down slightly to hold it there. Hold it there for 30 to 60 seconds. As strange as it may seem, you will most likely start to feel a positive emotional shift.

Now, just take this pen or pencil, and "trap" it between your nose and your upper lip, by scrunching up your top lip, so you can hold it against the bottom of your nose. Hold it there for 30 seconds. If you did the previous exercise before trying this one, you'll be blown away by how fast the good feelings start to reverse.

Mother Theresa believed that peace begins with a smile, and after you experience the simple but profound contrast in feelings when you do these two exercises with the pen, you may find yourself starting to view her belief much more seriously.

After a decade of studying accelerated methods for changing human behavior, this was the one area that I had personally never studied as much as I should have. Once I started experimenting with these facial exercises, it became obvious to me how much of my day did not involve a smile. It's not that this made me un-happy, but it certainly limited the intensity and duration my good feelings. Learning to smile, as a way of being, will make literally anything else you do more pleasurable.

Among other things, smiling signals pain killing *endorphins* and immune system boosters like *T-cells*. It also lowers the stress hormones *cortisol, adrenalin* and *noradrenalin,* and produces hormones that stabilize and even lower the blood pressure.

Frowning, on the other hand, increases blood pressure, weakens the immune system, and fuels depression and anxiety. The opposite of what you can accomplish with a smile.

Sometimes, in response to hearing about the benefits of smiling, people will say, "Okay, I can force it, I can make a fake smile, but what's the point? It's not real." Fortunately, research has shown that even a "fake" smile can trick the brain into triggering the aforementioned changes in your biochemistry, just at lower levels.

You see, simple changes in facial expressions bring about profound changes in the emotions that we are experiencing, and this in turn sculpts the moods we operate from most consistently. And, on top of that, our expressions communicate powerfully to others. So powerfully, in fact, others may even begin to feel what we are feeling. That *can* be very useful. However, unless you are using this methodically and with intention, you may be inviting them to experience feelings other than those that would be most beneficial.

When I was about 17 years old, I was standing in a parking lot one night taking with some friends. There was girl that I had seen around for years, but had never spoken to before, that happened to be in the group that night. I initiated a conversation with her, and for several minutes we were just chatting away, when suddenly, she said "You know, I always thought you were a real jerk, but you're actually a really nice guy!"

I was speechless. I had never spoken to this girl before in my life. "How in the hell could she have thought I was a jerk, she didn't even know me?" I wondered.

Here's what had happened. When I was a teenager, I used to fight a lot. I became addicted to the feeling of winning a fight. Problem was, it was a short lived feeling, and I had to constantly be re-creating those feelings by winning another fight. I had boxed myself into a tight little trap. I had a reputation of being a "tough guy", and as poor as my self-esteem had been for some time, it felt pretty good to recognized, even if it was for winning a fight.

The more in love I fell with the recognition, the more desperate I became to keep the right to be viewed as a "tough guy." Over time, I had taken on the identity of a "tough guy." I had the walk, the look, the gestures, the voice, all of the things that communicated, "I'm tough!" What I didn't know, however, was that not everyone perceived my communication the same way.

Back to the girl in the parking lot. Since she had never talked to me before, but had seen me several times a week each year, (I grew up in a small town) the only communication she had the chance to process, was saying, "I'm tough!" When she would see me, she would just get a bad feeling about me. For her, this feeling translated to "He's a jerk!" Having had the opportunity to talk to her in recent years, I asked her one day to describe what she had felt in those times she would see me before we had ever officially met. She said, "You know, I'd see you, and I'd just feel tense and aggressive, and not being an aggressive person, I just didn't like that feeling."

Why did my aggressiveness make *her* feel aggressive? One likely explanation is something called a mirror neuron. Mirror neurons cause us to mimic, and thus experience, much of what we observe. These neurons literally "mirror" the behavior of the person we are observing, causing our physiology to experience that which we are watching. In1992, an Italian scientist named Giacomo Rizzolatti was studying the brains of the macaque, a certain species of monkey. While watching the pre-motor area of the brain they observed something interesting. Not only did this area of the monkey's brain light up when the *monkey* was reaching for an object, it also lit up when watching *another monkey*, or even *one of the researchers* reaching for an object. Their brain had mentally imitated the very same gesture.

Keep that in mind when you are choosing who you hang out with. You are *always* mirroring the behavior and attitudes of those around you. Other people are always influencing the way you feel; you can pick up some pretty bad habits, just because of the people you spend time with.

Do the people you spend the most time with feel and behave the way you want to? Are they living in a way that would support them in the achievement of a goal similar to yours? If not, you may want to re-examine who you are spending the most time hanging out with. I don't think I can over emphasize the importance of this. It's a critical factor, and if you choose to, you can now use this awareness to bring the people into your life that can help you get to the next level.

CHAPTER 49:

DONNIE & MARIE AND A BIG ROUND OF APPLAUSE

"Laughter is higher than all pain."

-Elbert Hubbard

I'll never forget the first time I discovered that not everything is what it looks like on the surface, or in this case, what it sounds like. In 1978, my parents sent me to a track and field summer camp at Brigham Young University in Utah. I stayed with some family friends that had lived right across the street from us in Trenton before moving to Provo, Utah. Bob and Dee Johnson didn't have kids of their own, so they "adopted" me, treating me like the son they had never had. After moving to Utah, Bob had taken a job as the assistant coach for the BYU baseball team, and Dee, who had been in broadcasting at a small radio station in Trenton, had taken a position with Osmond Studio's. This was at the height of the Donnie and Marie Show's popularity, so when I got the chance to go with Dee for a behind the scenes tour of Osmond studios at 12 years old, you can imagine my level of excitement!

It was almost overwhelming to go into Donnie and Marie Osmond's personal dressing rooms, and to have Jimmy Osmond give me an autographed copy of his book *The Great Brain* which was actually a movie he had starred in as the main character. Jimmy was only three years older than me, but was already a movie star and very successful performer. I was in awe.

One day, while at the Studio, I was walking through where the audience members would sit during the taping of the show. I noticed that up above the seats, there were lights that said, "Applause" and "Laugh." I couldn't believe it. I looked at the tour guide and said, "You mean you tell the people when to laugh and when to clap?" I wondered why they didn't just let the people laugh if they thought it was funny.

I didn't know it at the time, but the laughter I heard on some of my favorite T.V. shows, (The *Andy Griffith Show*, *Gilligan's Island*, and *Leave it to Beaver*) didn't come from people in a live audience. The laughter I was hearing when I watched those shows came from pre-recorded "laugh tracks." Why did the producers insert these "laugh tracks"? I mean, if it was funny, we would surely laugh by ourselves, wouldn't we? The television producers knew then, and I know now, that when we hear laughter, we are more likely to laugh and will actually think something is funnier.

The networks knew this was a powerful key for getting people to tune into their program every week. Did it work? You bet it did. One of the first shows to revolt, and air without the laugh tracks in the 60's, crashed within a few episodes.

I've actually had the opportunity to watch some of my favorite shows with the laugh tracks removed, and I can tell you, they just weren't as funny.

How can you structure your day so that you can spend more time laughing? What situations could you lighten up a bit, by adding a background of humor? Start adding "laugh tracks" to your life and see what happens.

CHAPTER 50:

THE REASON MONA LISA SMILES

"Before you put on a frown, make absolutely sure there are no smiles available."

-Jim Beggs

While laughing triggers a cascade of useful physiological and chemical responses, laughter also contracts the same muscles in our face as a genuine smile. And as you know, putting a smile on our face is very beneficial.

I want to share something with you I learned while in Thailand in the early 90's; something called the "Inner Smile." Just relax your face, and simply let a very subtle, almost "Mona Lisa" like smile ease onto your face, and just hold that for a bit. Just enjoy the sense of ease and comfort that quickly starts flooding your body. Now, suddenly, shift your face into a scowl or frown, and notice the immediate shift in how you feel and your energy level. Wouldn't it be a shame to have a million dollars in the bank, but no checkbook or debit card to get it some of it out? I might suggest that it's even worse to have a brain that will release such powerful feelings of happiness, and to never smile. A smile is to happiness, what a checkbook is to a million dollars in the bank.

Does it seem like we've already talked about this? If you see something more than once, allow that to be a signal of how important it is to your productivity.

CHAPTER 51:

VOTED MOST LIKELY TO BE HAPPY

"Sometimes your joy is the source of your smile, but sometimes your smile can be the source of your joy."

-Thich Nhat Hanh

Funny man of the silent movies, Charlie Chaplin, once said that "Life is a tragedy when viewed up close and a comedy in the long shot" Chaplin was reflecting on the power of getting some emotional distance on those things perceived as problems. What role, if any, does a smile have in creating this emotional distance? Don't we have to be happy *before* we smile?

I saw a sign in a doctor's office waiting room that said, "They do not sing because they are happy, they are happy because they sing." The same can be said of a smile, "They are not smiling because they are happy, they are happy because they are smiling.

Dr. Dacher Kelter of the University of California has been studying college yearbook photos for over forty years. What he's discovered is just one more reason to start smiling more and more each day. Keltner found that those who had the biggest and most genuine smiles in their year book photos were on average, much happier in the years after graduating than those who weren't smiling. What do I mean by "genuine smile"? Over a hundred years ago, Duchenne de Boulogne, a neurologist from France, identified the muscles in our face that contract with a spontaneous happy and genuine smile. In short, a smile that is born from real heartfelt emotions includes the contraction of muscles around the eyes called *orbicularis oculi*. Paul Ekman's research confirmed Duchennes previous claim that most people could not *voluntarily* contract this muscle.

That's why on some level, we can so easily tell a "fake" smile in someone else. In a forced or fake smile, the contraction of the *orbicularis oculi,* remains inactive, and the smile is less than genuine in appearance.

How do we create a genuine smile? When you vividly recall a pleasant or joyous experience, so much so that you once again experience the good feelings that go with the memory, the genuine smile will occur spontaneously. When I remember rocking my daughter to sleep when she was about two years old, I don't have to "try" and smile; when I deeply access this memory, it's just there. Take a few moments today, and scan through your past for one or two memories that you can instantly use to create the kind of feelings that would generate a beautiful yearbook photo.

CHAPTER 52:

A DIFFERENT KIND OF BODY LANGUAGE

"The illiterate of the future are not those that cannot read or write. They are those that cannot learn, unlearn, relearn."

-Alvin Toffler

Thomas Hanna was the founder of the field of Somatics, and the director of the Novato Institute for Somatic Research and Training. In a nutshell, Somatics deals with the movement of our physical body and its relationship to our overall mental and physical health. Hanna often referred to what he called *somatic amnesia* or *sensory motor amnesia*. This is the neurological process where the brain "forgets" how to control muscles and how they relax.

Certain kinds of accidents, injuries, trauma and stress can lead to *habituated muscular dysfunction*, or the habit of using our body in a less than resourceful way. We develop an inability to voluntarily control or relax muscles. In other words, sometimes the posture we have created requires that certain muscles stay contracted constantly.

Through systematic, precise movement exercises, the *sensory-motor tracts* of the brain and muscles are freed from these involuntary contractions, and are then taught to regain voluntary control. *Somatic amnesia* really comes down to simply not being aware of the position or feeling of our body. Awareness is the starting point.

The key in teaching the body to naturally and automatically change our posture and alignment is to *first* become aware of how it feels when we are in a less that useful position, or are using our physiology in a way that does not support our physical comfort and emotional states.

I want to take a moment to remind you that this works both ways. Our thoughts and what we're thinking about will eventually shift our physiology, and, our physiology, or the way we are using our body will powerfully influence what we are thinking. But how much will it change?

In one study, researchers actually altered the amount of physical energy people were able to put forth with their physical body, by introducing a few simple thoughts. John Bargh, Mark Chen and Lara Burrows, gave thirty psychology students little word puzzles to complete. 50% of the students had puzzles with words like, retired, old, careful, shaky, and ancient. The other half worked on puzzles with more neutral words. After completing the puzzle, they were free to get up and go on with their day.

Unbeknownst to them, however, the researchers were secretly timing how long it took each student to walk back to the elevator. Those who had worked on the puzzles with words related to *older* people took more time to get to the elevator. By seeing these few words related to the elderly, their brains had been primed in such a way that their behavior changed. They actually walked slower because of what they read.

Clearly, our thoughts can and do influence how we feel. The other side of this equation is that the way we use our bodies can determine how resourceful we think and feel.

How do you use your body? Are you stiff and inflexible? If so, the goal of working to increase your flexibility and range of motion can work wonders. As you free up your body, you'll also be freeing your mind. Not just metaphorically, but literally.

There are many good forms of treatment to bring your flexibility back to something closer to what it was ten years ago. Is it just a coincidence that as people age and their body begins to stiffen, that their thinking becomes more rigid as well? I don't think so. Give this reverse approach a try. At the very least, you'll find that it doesn't take you as long to get out of bed, and that it doesn't hurt quite as much when you do.

CHAPTER 53:

EYE SPY PRODUCTIVE FEELINGS

"The coach who goes home and doesn't think about the game he just lost is bound to repeat his mistakes."

-Keith Cooper

It's often said that they eyes are the window to the soul, and while I won't attempt to prove or disprove that idea, I will say that the eyes *are* another key part of altering how we feel; more specifically, the location of our eyes and where we are looking.

The co-developers of NLP, or Neuro-Lingusitic Programming discovered that we access different areas of our brain more efficiently when we move our eyes to locations associated with those areas of processing. As a general rule (and yes, there are some exceptions to this) when we are making pictures in our mind, either consciously or unconsciously, we look up to the left, up to the right, or sometimes just stare straight ahead. When we are looking down and to the right, we are usually accessing a feeling. Finally, when looking down to our left, we are most likely talking to ourselves inside our head. There are other locations, and far more to the topic of eye movements, but this is enough to understand the following example.

A lady once called me and said she was having a problem. She said "When I get into church each Sunday, and start to listen to the sermon, I just start crying, and I can't stop crying in church." When I asked her about the last time this happened, her eyes immediately went down and to the right, and then quickly darted over down to the left, and within a few seconds, the tears were flowing, and she didn't have any idea why. Keep in mind that these movements were completely outside of her awareness. All she was aware of was the "bad" feeling that she felt when the crying started.

Knowing that most people access feelings by moving their eyes down and to the right, and that when people are talking to themselves on the inside, they often move them down to the left, I had a good idea what the structure of her problem was. She was accessing some feeling or emotion, and then saying something to herself about it, and because it led to her crying, it was a safe bet that the feeling she was accessing, and what she was saying to herself *about* this feeling, probably wasn't something particularly useful.

I didn't need to know *what* the feeling was, or *what* she was saying in her mind about it. Changing people is often as simple of finding out how they make the problem work, and then getting them to STOP, by giving them something else to do. Sometimes it really is that simple. All I needed to do was to get her to *do something else*.

I had her move her eyes up to the right, and imagine a picture or image of herself out in her garden, because I knew she loved working in her garden, and would therefore find it easy to think of images related to her plants and flowers. To make sure this was going to work, I had her run through her old pattern a few times, and when the previously uncontrollable tears would start to flow, I'd say "Now", and that was her cue to move her eyes up and to the right.

When she did this, her tears dried up faster than a drop of water on a hot summer sidewalk. We then rehearsed the experience of being in church, and feeling like she was going to start crying, and at this point, she would immediately move her eyes up to the right. All it took was about fifteen rehearsals to make this automatic. She never again cried in church unless she wanted to in some appropriate situation.

Did she have to go through years of psychoanalysis? No. Did she have to get to the "root" of what she was thinking about that was making her cry? No. All she needed to do was figure out how she was triggering the tears, and then, by simply changing how she was using her body, (and therefore her mind) she instantly created a different result. I saw her one time, and the session took fifty-five minutes. When you are using the right tools, change is usually quick and simple. There are some exceptions, but for the most part, I've found people can change faster than they thought they had ever thought possible. Once you know the combination to the lock, "click", it opens effortlessly. Try using the wrong numbers and you simply wind up frustrated and tired.

CHAPTER 54:

THE SPIN ZONE

"If Casey Stengal were alive today, he'd be spinning in his grave."

-Ralph Kiner

Let's talk about another way we can use our body to quickly change how we feel. Do you remember when you were a kid, and you used to go outside, look up at the sky, and then just spin around until you fell down?

As it turns out, this is a brilliant way to stimulate the brain, and even as adults, we can benefit from it immensely. Our inner ear, or what's called the vestibular system, is stimulated when we engage in spinning type movements.

Dr. Lyelle Palmer of *Winona State University* has documented magnificent gains in both attention and reading among school children who were asked to perform spinning movements each day. In fact, in a study in Seattle Washington, even though the district reading scores fell by 2% in the general population, in those children who were taking part in frequent dance activities, (that involved spinning) researchers witnessed scores rise by 13% in six months.

The spinning sends electrical impulses into the brain, which then stimulates the limbic system. This has a positive impact on pleasure and learning, while simultaneously causing your brain waves to shift to those that correspond to pleasure and rest.

So you might be thinking, "What's this have to do with increasing my productivity?" Our feelings are processed through our brain and nervous system, so it only makes sense that the more efficiently we are able to use this "wiring" if you will, the more effective we will be at nearly anything else we want to do.

I stand in the middle of the living room each morning, and spin around about ten times to the left, and then ten times to the right. It's kind of like a physical cup of coffee. Will you join me for coffee?

CHAPTER 55:

STAND UP AND BE COUNTED

"Experience is the best teacher, but a fool will learn from no other."

-Ben Franklin

Physical movement is instrumental in the learning process. The traditional set up of classrooms all across the nation, all but guarantees that students will be functioning below their potential. We were we told, "Sit in your seat, and be quiet." Could it be that this was not the sound advice many teachers thought it was, and worse yet, that many teachers still do?

Dr. Max Verycruyssen of the *University of Southern California* believes that blood flow and oxygen to the brain have a great deal to do with how well we learn and how we feel.

By simply asking a student to stand up, he found that their heart rate would increase by ten beats per minute, thus driving more blood and oxygen to the brain. The net result? The students attention was aroused, and their ability to process information increased by 5-20 %. By standing up they were getting about 15% more oxygen to their brain.

Long before I had ever discovered this research, I knew this intuitively. My best ideas have always come to me while I'm running. Look, we all know we need to exercise anyway, right? I've always felt that if I could learn something of value *while* I was exercising, that I'm really getting as much value as I possibly can out of that particular block of time. Thinking like this is the heart and soul of becoming more productive.

CHAPTER 56:

A JAW DROPPING EXPERIENCE

"In general, any form of exercise, if pursued continuously, will help train us in perseverance. Long-distance running is particularly good training in perseverance."

-Mao Tse-Tung

Neuroscientists discovered that when we exercise, we initiate the release of BDNF, or what's called *brain derived neurotrophic factor*. This naturally produced chemical radically increases the ability of the neurons to communicate with each other, and therefore, significantly increases our rate of learning and our ability to recall and remember. Learning and memory are chemical events.

What about the impact of stress on learning? Does the amount of tension we have in our body impact how effectively we can learn? Thirty-Nine adults took part in a study at *Stanford University*, at the School of Medicine. One group was trained to relax every muscle in their body, prior to the memory training. The other group just took the memory training. Not too surprisingly, the relaxation group scored 25% higher on a test that was given later.

While it may come as a surprise, any conversation about relaxing or decreasing stress needs to include discussion of the jaw muscles. Nearly 50% of the nerve connections that pass into your brain from your body pass through the jaw. By simply relaxing the jaw muscles, you can create a rather profound difference in your level of relaxation.

Shortly after my wife and I were married, she was watching me play my electric guitar, and when I was done she said, "That sounded pretty cool, but why do you make all of those faces?"

I'm sure she could have cared less *why* I was making those faces,

I think that was just her way of saying, "You look stupid when you do that!" Little did she know, however, was that I had good reason for my facial contortions. Eddie Van Halen has long been my favorite guitar player, and one of the things I had always noticed, not only in him, but in most any other guitar player I watched, was that their facial expressions would change as they played. Interestingly enough, even though the expressions changed, their jaw muscles were *always* loose.

If you watch someone who is just learning to play guitar, especially if they are having challenges, they'll almost always have a clenched jaw. Even though they improve technically over time, they establish the habit of clenching their jaw when they play, and this keeps them from ever being able to access that "zone" where things become effortless.

My playing went to a whole new level when I started to watch videos of great guitar players, and then started to mimic their facial expressions. I had an immediate shift in how smooth and relaxed I was, and as a result, I not only sounded better, but I just enjoyed it a whole lot more.

Think of unnecessary tension as something like a governor that keeps a car from going over a certain speed. Several times a day, do a quick check of how relaxed your jaw muscles are, and if there is still room for more relaxation, just let go a little more. It will never cease to amaze me how something as simple as how relaxed we keep our jaw muscles can make such a difference in how much enjoyment we get out of life, and how efficient, productive or effective we become.

CHAPTER 57:

HO'OPONOPONO WHO?

"The current perception I get from the evening news is that the world is dominated by human failure, crime, catastrophe, corruption, and tragedy. We are all tuning in to see how the human mind is evolving, but the media keeps hammering home the opposite, that the human mind is mired in darkness and folly."

-Deepak Chopra

I must admit, when I first picked up Joe Vitale's book *Zero Limits: The Secret Hawaiian System for Wealth, Health, Peace and More,* it was pure curiosity that drove the purchase. I had read a story about how Vitale had teamed up with a master teacher of something called Ho'oponopono, an ancient Hawaiian healing art. The master teacher was a gentleman who had reportedly healed the patients in the Hawaii State Hospital, not by working with *them,* but by working on *himself.* While I tend to be skeptical by nature, I refuse to come to a conclusion until I have examined both sides of something. Vitale had me hooked. I bought the book and headed for home.

I'm all about results. If I do something, and it works for me, I'm not going to let the fact that the theory it operates on runs counter to one of my long held beliefs. In his book, Vitale tells of how the master told him that by repeating the words *I'm sorry, please forgive me,* and *I love you,* his energy would shift from within, and he would be healing any obstacles between himself and the "Divine."

The part of me that thinks like a scientist thought "There is no evidence showing that repeating any known words will heal anyone, or help them connect with the Divine." The part of me that likes to find things that work said "There's no evidence that concludes this *doesn't* work either."

I decided, that for the next few days, when I was having a conversation with someone, when they were speaking I would silently repeat "I'm sorry, please forgive me, I love you." Clearly, I was going to feel silly, but no one would know...or would they?

I trusted Joe Vitale. After all, 48 hours after having implemented one of the strategies I found in his book *There's a Customer Born Every Minute: P.T. Barnum's 10 Rings of Power for Fame, Fortune and Building an Empire*, I made an extra $1,200.

Almost immediately, strange things started to happen after I started silently reciting these "magic" words while listening to someone speak. Suddenly, people were telling me things, that, under previous circumstances, I would have to work really hard to bring forth. But something was happening to me too. I live on a beautiful farm in North Missouri with my wife, daughter and several farm animals. We have 12 cats, 2 dogs, 14 chickens and a blue rat. It was as if I had started oozing some pheromone that was causing the brains of my fur and feather covered friends to be flooded with the "I want to be close to Vince!" chemical. They followed me everywhere I went.

Could this be useful? Would being able to cause people to feel wonderful when they are near you be helpful in business? At home?

Why does this happen? Look, we know that both our brain and our heart generate an electromagnetic field. My hunch is that when we are thinking something that is generating a "good' feeling, we somehow alter that field. Given the fact that research on "self talk" shows that most people spend a great deal of time having "negative" conversations in their head, it should come as no surprise that people want to be near anyone who can help them out of this self-defeating loop. When we take the time to actually shift our "fields" or "vibes" to something that makes *us* feel good, we are also inviting *others* to feel good as well. We all have an impact on one another.

I would urge you to get *Zero Limits: The Secret Hawaiian System for Wealth, Health, Peace and More*, or any other book by Joe Vitale. While you may or may not agree with the theory of Ho'oponopono, if you'll simply repeat those few simple words over and over again, you'll experience something that I know you'll find beneficial.

CHAPTER 58:

MY WIFE CONFIRMED MY FEAR-THANK GOODNESS SHE WAS WRONG

"I think the next best thing to solving a problem is finding some humor in it."
-Frank A. Clark

Several years ago I had just finished giving a keynote presentation to a group of emergency room physicians. My wife had attended this particular presentation, and was present in the audience that evening. After the evenings activities were through, we jumped into our car and started for the home. Suddenly, my wife's voice pierced the mental fog I had drifted into as I listened to Blue Oyster Cult's *Don't Fear the Reaper* on the radio. "Honey" she said, "Can I tell you something?" I had never found anything she had to say that was prefaced by this question inspiring, and this would be no exception.

"Sure" I quipped, "What's on your mind?" She hesitantly responded. "Your presentation was great, as usual. They were captivated by your stories, and almost everyone was taking notes, it was obviously a hit." Then came the death blow. "But honey, you're not funny!"

My mind was spinning wildly. She had just confirmed my worst fear, my fear that I wasn't funny. I had never felt like I was funny. I admired the ability of those who were funny with little effort. As much I admired it in others, though, I had never been able to pull it off. The "sting" I had felt from her words hinted powerfully at the accuracy of her observation. She was right; I wasn't funny, not even a little bit.

Nearly every book I had ever read about professional speaking said that you should "get them laughing" early in your presentation. However, none of them had ever taken the time to explain *how* to be funny. There were no strategies, formulas, or templates in any of these books, just a variation of ambiguous instruction that said "be funny."

Then, I picked up Tom Antion's *Wake'em Up! How to use humor and other professional techniques to create alarmingly good business presentations.*

Chapter 13 of Tom's book is titled *Thirty-Four way's to be funny.* As it turns out, that's thirty three more than I had been painfully using to try and get a laugh. Perhaps the most important thing I learned from Tom Antion was that you have to find the method that works for you. Some people can successfully tell jokes to get an audience laughing. Others, for enough reasons to fill an entire book, will do irreparable damage when they try to invoke humor with a joke.

A favorite method of mine (one that I learned from Tom's book) is to use humorous quotes from other people, preferably *someone famous* that the listeners will be familiar with. See, if I tell you what someone else said, and you don't laugh, you simply didn't find *them* funny. The important thing at this point, is that, you haven't concluded that *I* wasn't funny. Even stranger, perhaps, the fact that I'm telling you something that someone famous once said, *will* significantly increase the probability of you finding it funny, especially if I can quote someone I know you admire and respect.

Borrowing one of the quotes offered in Tom's book, If I was on a sales presentation and a prospect tells me how many problems they have had with their current insurance company, with a grin on my face I could say "Mike, Abraham Lincoln once said 'When you've got an elephant by the hind legs and he is trying to run away, it's best to let him run." If Mike finds it funny, I have just loosened the "grip" of his current company, and I can now more effectively show him why we are the better choice. If he doesn't, well, he just thinks *Lincoln's* comment wasn't particularly funny.

The humor technique I clearly get the most mileage from, however, is *self-deprecating* or *self-effacing* humor. Self-deprecation is poking fun at one of your own obvious "flaws."

Almost everyone we meet has some degree of what we would refer to as "low" self-esteem. Therefore, in any audience or group of people we are talking to, whether it is delivering a keynote presentation to five hundred or a briefing to just a few co-workers in the lunch room, we can trust that several of those present will have self-esteem "issues." Chances are good, that they perceive us to have some important trait that they are lacking, whether it's true or not. Then, to top things off, if we are in a leadership position, they also perceive us as an authority figure. This combination of a perceived trait imbalance *and* our position of authority or status can generate deep feelings of resentment.

While I'm far from being bald, it's obvious to anyone who's not legally blind that I have a receding hair line. I sometimes tell the story of how my five year old daughter was climbing on my back, and pulling on my ears, when I felt her tiny little finger tracing a symmetrical pattern on my head. I then tell how she leaned over far enough so she could see our reflection in the living room mirror and said "Look Daddy, you have that *thing* on your head like the McDonald's sign" referencing the "M" pattern on the front of my once hair covered scalp. This always gets a laugh, but more importantly, it causes people to think "Hey, this guy is human; he isn't perfect; he doesn't think he's perfect, and is insecure about some part of his life like everyone else.

One important note on using self-deprecating humor: Use it like spice; us it very sparingly. In small doses it builds rapport and trust. Used excessively, just like any spice used in excess, it leaves a bad taste in the mouth of other people. Remember, people want to listen to people who are confident and competent, and when you *continually* run yourself down, you convey neither.

If you, like me, have found yourself thinking "I'm not funny", realize that you've probably been suffering from a very limited tool box of humor techniques, and according to Tom Antion, there are at least thirty-four ways to approach being funny. Find the methods that work best for you, and enjoy having others slide into a more receptive state of mind when you get them to laugh with ease. Does my wife think I'm funny now? Not necessarily, but most everyone else does, and I have Tom Antion to thank for that.

CHAPTER 59:

IT'S HOW THE STORY'S TOLD THAT MATTERS MOST

"If you call forth what is in you, it will save you. If you do not call forth what is in you, it will destroy you."

  -Gospel of Saint Thomas

Soon after starting as an insurance agent in the mid 80's, I was introduced to Zig Ziglar. I was immediately captivated by his storytelling, convinced that no one could tell a better story than Zig. The stories that Zig told were meant to do one thing, and they did it well; they slid the real message right into long term storage, leaving us with a vital new piece of knowledge, without even realizing at the time, that we were learning anything. I thought Zig was the best...until I listened to a tape of Hank Trisler.

Listening to Hank Trisler was like listening to the guys who used to sit around the pot-bellied stove in Bones Lionberger's army surplus store on those cold January afternoons when I was a kid. There was no self-editing; there was no inner analyzing of something before it was said, and most importantly, no one was rounding the edges off of their emotions when they were telling a story. Their stories had guts. I never heard a watered down story around that glowing stove. While the content of those stories for a ten year old may have been questionable, they were an example of how to tell a captivating story.

Hank Trisler was the first person I had ever heard that could tell a raw fireside story that was also clean enough to tell to a class of 8 year olds in Sunday school. How did he do it? I think one key was that Hank wasn't trying to impress anyone. He was telling the story he knew would ultimately be heard by thousands on audio tape, just like he might tell it to an old uncle, sitting on the back porch after gorging at a family dinner.

Maybe you have suffered through listening to one of those "polished" studio perfect audio programs. You know, the ones where the cadence and tempo are consistent with someone reading a script? The ones that are "careful" not to let their emotions get too "wild" for fear that the more conservative listeners might be offended. No matter how valuable the content of a program like this, you'll probably never remember it when you need it. Something being read in an even, and "perfectly "paced tempo just won't stick. It's just not presented in the way the brain processes best.

It's long been rumored that when Gene Autry was trying to make the big time, he worked very hard at losing his Texas accent. However, it wasn't until he decided to belt out his songs with that big, bold Texas sound that things really took off. Gene stopped trying to please everyone, and started giving the world the Gene Autry he had always been- and they loved it. Sincerity feels good, and basks others in warming rays like nothing else can.

Did I learn any useful sales techniques from Hank Trisler's tape set, *No Bull Selling?* Yes I did. But what Hank really taught me paid off bigger than I could have imagined. It was probably never Hank's intention to teach the art of an amazingly honest story, but isn't that when some of the best lessons are learned? Twenty-two years after I first heard Hank speak, he's still going strong. I would urge you to model Hank's masterful story telling by listening, as I did, to the colorful and enjoyable tales he tells.

Have you been squashing down the best part of yourself, for fear others might think you are "over the top"? There will never be another you, so you might as well be the best you, you possibly can. I think you'll find, as I have, that you can't give the best you have to offer when you put a "governor" on what you have to offer. If you are from Georgia and have that wonderful Georgia accent, nothing sounds worse than trying to talk like someone from Maine; it just won't come across in a favorable way. Hey, there are enough people from Maine to talk with *that* accent. Let the unique aspects of who you are become your signature. People will feel more comfortable with you, because *you* are comfortable with you.

In Closing:

After you have read *The Productivity Epiphany* once, just put it down somewhere for a couple weeks. Then, every few days, simply pick it back up and read it for another 5-10 minutes. You'll get something new every time for months to come. Things that weren't clear to you before will be. Things that were clear the first time around will become clearer. Let your mind work; this book is just a tool to trigger the brilliance within.

Enjoy.

About the Author

Vincent Harris is a body language expert and the President and CEO of Harris Research International.

Vince's uncanny ability to detect the subtle, but vital communication signals offered by others, and then use that information to help them to rapidly achieve their goals, prompted one psychologist to give him the title of *The Human Whisperer.*

As an international speaker, trainer and consultant, he teaches men and women around the world to maximize their performance using leading edge methods for making accelerated behavioral changes.

BIBLIOGRAPHY

Andreas, Connirae. (2004). *NLP and Advanced Language Patterns*. Boulder, CO: NLP Comprehensive

Andreas, Steve & Faulkner, Charles. (1996). *The New Technology of Achievement*. New York, NY: Harper Collins

Antion, Tom. (1999). *Wake'em Up! How to use humor and other professional techniques to create alarmingly good business presentations.* Landover Hills, MD: Anchor Publishing.

Austin, Andrew T. (2007). *The Rainbow Machine: Tales from a Neurolinguist's Journal.* Boulder, CO: Real People Press

Byrne, Rhonda. (2006). *The Secret, DVD*. London, England. Atria Books

Canfield, Jack. (2005). *The Success Principles: How to Get from Where You Are to Where You Want to Be.* New York, NY: Collins.

Chandler, Steve. (2004). *100 Ways to Motivate Yourself: Change Your Life Forever.* Franklin Lakes, NJ: Career Press

Childre, Doc & Martin, Howard. (2000). *The HeartMath Solution: The Institute of HeartMath's Revolutionary Program for Engaging the Power of the Heart's Intelligence. San Francisco, CA: HarperOne*

Ekman, Paul. (2003). *Emotions Revealed: Recognizing Faces and Feelings to Improve Communication and Emotional Life.* New York, NY: Henry Holt and Company, LLC

Goleman, Daniel. (1995). *Emotional Intelligence: Why it can matter more than IQ.* New York, NY: Bantam Dell

Gottman, John. (1995). *Why Marriages Succeed or Fail :And How You Can Make Yours Last.* New York, NY: Simon & Schuster

Hall, Michael L. (1996). *Dragon Slaying: Dragons into Princes.* Grand Junction, CO: E.T. Publications

Hanna, Thomas. (2004). *Somatics: Reawakening the Mind's Control of Movement, Flexibility, and Health.* Cambridge, MA: De Capo Books

Hartley, Gregory, & Karinch, Maryann. (2005). *How to Spot a Liar: Why People Don't Tell the Truth and How You Can Catch Them.* Franklin

Lakes, NJ: Career Press

Hogan, Kevin. (1996). *The Psychology of Persuasion: How to Persuade Others to Your Way of Thinking. Gretna, LA: Pelican Publishing*

Hogan, Kevin. (2008). *The Secret Language of Business: How to Read Anyone in 3 Seconds or Less. Hoboken, NJ: Wiley*

Howard, Vernon. (2001). *Psycho-Pictography: The New Way to Use The Miracle Power of Your Mind.* New Life Foundation

Knowles, Eric S. & Linn, Jay A. (2003). *Resistance and Persuasion.* Mahwah, NJ: Lawrence Erlbaum

Lieberman, David J. (2005). *How to Change Anybody.* New York, NY: St. Martin's Press

Lieberman, David J. (2007). *You Can Read Anyone: Never Be Fooled, Lied to or Taken Advantage of Again.* Lakewood, NJ: Viter Press

Lindstrom, Martin. (2008). *Buy.ology: Truth and Lies About Why We Buy* .New York, NY: Doubleday

Maxwell, John C. (2005). *Today Matters: 12 Daily Practices to Guarantee Tomorrow's Success.* New York, NY: Center Street

Mortensen, Kurt W. (2004). *Maximum Influence: The 12 Universal Laws of Power Persuasion.* New York, NY: Amacom

Neill, Michael. (2006). *You Can Have What You Want: Proven Strategies for Inner and Outer Success.* Hayhouse

Nightingale, Earl. (2007). *The Strangest Secret. www.Bnpublishing.com*

Pease, Allen & Pease, Barbara. (2006). *The Definitive Book of Body Language.* New York, NY: Bantam

Reiman, Tonya. (2007). *The Power of Body Language.* New York, NY: Pocket Books

Reiss, Steven. (2002). *Who Am I? The 16 Basic Desires that Motivate and Define Our Personalities.* New York, NY: Berkley Trade

Rubino, Joe. (2003). *Restore Your Magnificence: A Life-Changing Guide to Reclaiming Your Self-Esteem* .Brooklyn, NY: Vision Works Publishing

St.Clair, Carmen, & Bostic, Grinder, John. (2001).*Whispering In The Wind.* Scotts Valley, CA: J&C Enterprises

Tracy, Brian. (2007). *Eat That Frog! 21 Great Ways to Stop Procrastinating and Get More Done in Less Time.* San Francisco, CA:Berrett-Koelhler Publishers, Inc.

Trisler, Hank. (1986). *No Bull Selling: Winning Sales Strategy from America's Super Salesman*. New York, NY: Random House Audio Publishing Group

Vitale, Joe. (2006). *There's a Customer Born Every Minute: P.T. Barnum's 10 Rings of Power for Fame, Fortune and Building an Empire* .Hoboken, NJ: Wiley

Vitale, Joe. & Len, Ihaleakala Hew. (2007). *Zero Limits: The Secret Hawaiian System for Wealth, Health, Peace and More*. Hoboken, NJ: Wiley

VINCENT HARRIS

SPEAKER, TRAINER, SEMINAR LEADER

Vincent Harris is arguably one of the most exciting professional speakers on the circuit today, capturing the attention of audience members and leaving them wanting more.

His keynote speeches, workshops and seminars are described as "uplifting, entertaining, inspirational, and extremely informative." His audiences include Fortune 500 companies and virtually every size of business and association.

Call today for information on booking Vince to speak at your next meeting.

It's About Time – How to eliminate procrastination, ignite motivation and get things done.

Facing Changes by Changing Faces – How to use the secrets of altering how you move your body to instantly reduce stress and access peak performance states.

Outstanding Customer Service – How to utilize verbal and non-verbal communication to create happier clients and customers.

Advanced Body Language – How to become a person of influence and use your non-verbal communication to communicate with precision.

Vince will customize his talk for you and your specific needs. Visit Harris Research International at WWW.VINCEHARRIS.COM for more information, or call 660-204-4088 today for more information.

Breinigsville, PA USA
11 September 2009
223941BV00001B/66/P